T0318466

Influencing Health

Influencing Health
A Comprehensive Guide to Working with Online Influencers

Amelia Burke-Garcia, PhD

A PRODUCTIVITY PRESS BOOK

First edition published in 2019
by Routledge/Productivity Press
52 Vanderbilt Avenue, 11th Floor New York, NY 10017
2 Park Square, Milton Park, Abingdon, Oxon OX14 4RN, UK

Printed on acid-free paper

International Standard Book Number-13: 978-0-367-24992-2 (Paperback)
International Standard Book Number-13: 978-0-367-26039-2 (Hardback)
International Standard Book Number-13: 978-0-429-29117-3 (eBook)

Library of Congress Cataloging-in-Publication Data

Names: Burke-Garcia, Amelia, author.
Title: Influencing health : a comprehensive guide to working with online influencers / Amelia Burke-Garcia.
Description: Boca Raton : Taylor & Francis, 2020. | "A Routledge title, part of the Taylor & Francis imprint, a member of the Taylor & Francis Group, the academic division of T&F Informa plc." | Includes bibliographical references. |
Identifiers: LCCN 2019011768 (print) | LCCN 2019018030 (ebook) | ISBN 9780429291173 (e-Book) | ISBN 9780367249922 (pbk. : alk. paper) | ISBN 9780367260392 (hardback : alk. paper)
Subjects: LCSH: Health promotion. | Health promotion—Philosophy.
Classification: LCC RA427.8 (ebook) | LCC RA427.8 .B87 2020 (print) | DDC 613.0285—dc23
LC record available at https://lccn.loc.gov/2019011768

Visit the Taylor & Francis Web site at
http://www.taylorandfrancis.com

and the CRC Press Web site at
http://www.crcpress.com

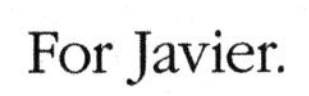

For Javier.

Contents

Foreword

Well over a decade ago, I heard about an NGO worker who had observed that in every town, village, or neighborhood she'd worked across the globe, there was always that one go-to woman who everyone in the community turned to for information, advice, or support.

Since then, I've always thought about bloggers and influencers as having much in common with that go-to person the NGO worker described—influencers are the source of information, tips, resources, and comfort for the communities they've worked so hard to nurture and build.

Over the years, I often ask influencers what draws them to their work, to their roles as community builders and content creators. One of the most common answers I get is that they come from a long line of helpers—family members and mentors who had strong ties and leadership roles in their neighborhoods and communities. Many had mothers or grandmothers who were teachers.

Influencer marketing is a term that has only recently entered the public lexicon; it's in the infancy stage as compared to other marketing tactics or strategies, but its most effective elements are as old, and tried and true, as time.

Think about how societies have historically built community and support, ways of sharing and connection—often the exercise is female driven: civic organizations, volunteerism, even quilting bees. Social media have been called the matriarchy of the Internet, and as Amelia has so expertly laid out through her research and interviews, it is!

When it comes to health and other important issues she and her family may face, women not only tend to be responsible for multiple balls in the air at one time, but they also are official connectors of the dots. That's a lot on her shoulders—she needs support, community, and help, always has and always will.

Amelia is an innovator in this space, and recognized early on that while working with influencers is new and cutting edge, it also taps deeply important and established needs and modes of communication. As an out-of-the-box thinker, Amelia also appreciates the infinite potential in influencer marketing, especially in the health field, not only in communicating but even as a mechanism for health data, insights, and research.

The best communicators are listeners, people who seek to understand, process what they hear, observe, and see, and then thoughtfully articulate their important, smart insights and critical thinking for the rest of us. Amelia has done exactly that with this book, providing a valuable roadmap for strategically implementing impactful and effective influencer marketing, with stories and anecdotes along the way, and building a compelling and vivid narrative for why influencer marketing matters and works.

By Cooper Munroe

CEO of The Motherhood Influencer Network

Testimonials

"In regularly working with Dr. Amelia Burke-Garcia on influencer marketing initiatives over the past several years, specifically for clients in the public health and wellness space, I've seen her passion and deep knowledge about the field and her work firsthand. She is one of the most well-organized, articulate, and strategic partners I've worked with, and unlike many marketing practitioners, she approaches social media and influencer work with the sound reasoning and trained eye of a great researcher. Dr. Burke-Garcia's dedication to matching the needs of her health clients with influencers who authentically engage their audiences on relevant topics, paired with her creativity, strong work ethic, and solutions-based approach to influencer marketing, have resulted directly in the success of one campaign after another. Within my company, we consider her a valued partner, and when she shares insights, ideas, and case studies from her work, others should sit up and take notice."

—Erin Olson

vice president, client services, The Motherhood influencer marketing agency.

"Strategic use of new methods for communicating health messages effectively in a digital-first world is critically important to ensuring that the right message gets shared and understood by the right person at the right moment. Unfortunately, there are not many authors with the relevant expertise needed to effectively guide strategic digital health communication.

Dr. Amelia Burke-Garcia, however, is one of the most well-qualified experts for guiding evolving digital health communication technologies, policies, and practices. Her vast experiences in digital health, coupled with her clear and conversational writing style, enable her to connect directly with readers to help them make informed choices about the best use of digital health communication. I highly recommend her important new book, *Influencing Health: A Comprehensive Guide to Working with Online Influencers*, to everyone studying or using digital health information systems."

—Gary L. Kreps, PhD
University Distinguished Professor of Communication, Director of the Center for Health and Risk Communication, George Mason University.

"Many of us who work in communication and marketing are easily swept up in the latest technology and social media channels without having the evidence to support of our decisions or a strategy to drive our activities. We are at a critical moment with influencer marketing, and this burgeoning field, which is expected to grow to a $10 billion industry by 2020, is desperately in need of supporting data, thoughtful research, and an evidence-based approach to guide today's brands and organizations. Dr. Amelia Burke-Garcia is the leading communication expert in this field, and her understanding of effective communication principles, published data on influencer marketing, and personal connections with many of today's leading influencers makes her the perfect person to write this book. My colleagues are repeatedly asking me for resources that provide best practices and tips on influencer marketing, and I am anxiously awaiting this book's publication. I'm confident it will serve as an invaluable resource to our field."

—Erin Norvell
Executive Director, Society for Health Communication; Founder and Principal Strategist, Digital Edge Communications.

Author

Dr. Amelia Burke-Garcia is an award-winning digital health communicator and researcher with more than 15 years of experience creating innovative and impactful digital interventions for health programs. Her work has included supporting flu vaccination by working with MeetUp groups across the country and partnering with the geolocation mobile application, Waze, to promote HIV testing. She has also been examining the role of influencers in health communication and research for more than a decade. She began her work with influencers in 2006 when she worked for Horizon Media, during which time she led what was then called Organic Marketing using fledgling networks of influencers to promote products and brands. She has expertly translated this experience to support and advance health-related programs, including running the first-ever Tweet-a-Thon with online mommy influencers promoting adolescent vaccination, as well as helping to lead a study examining the role of mommy bloggers in disseminating information about environmental risk factors for breast cancer. She has been a member of Merck's Global HPV Social Media and Communications Expert Input Forum, is the author of the S.O.C.I.A.L. framework for planning and evaluating digital campaigns, a member of the editorial board for Social Marketing Quarterly journal, a member of the Board of Directors for ShiftCon, the largest health and wellness influencer network in the United States, and has authored numerous book chapters and journals. She was also recently named to VeryWellHealth.com's list of ten Modern Female Innovators Shaking Up Health Care and received a 2014 Social Media Icon Award by PRNews Group. She holds a Ph.D. in communication from George Mason University, a Master's degree from Georgetown University, and a Bachelor's degree from McGill University.

Introduction

in·tro·duc·tion | /ˌintrəˈdəkSH(ə)n/ | noun
The action of introducing something.

Nearly 10 years ago, my grandmother was in hospice. She was 95, and after living a good long life, she was dying. Hospice is a funny thing. We make it sound like a physical place—a building you might pass on your way home from work. Often hospice centers are places that provide care for the sick, especially the terminally ill; however, hospice care can be provided wherever a patient calls home. So it is really not a physical place. Rather, it is a philosophy of care. As such, hospice aims to focus on the value of life and comfort at the end of that life.

My grandmother's hospice experience did not initially match this philosophy though. The nurses were not showing up and caring for her as they were supposed to. She was not getting the pain medication she needed. The attention being paid to her did not provide the comfort and dignity that hospice was supposed to ensure for the person dying.

During this time, I remember sitting around the kitchen table in my aunt and uncle's house with all the women of the family—my mom, my sister, all my cousins (they are almost all female), and my aunt. Everyone was complaining about my grandmother's situation and the lack of quality care she was getting at the hospice center.

I also remember feeling frustrated. I was frustrated by my grandmother's experience. I was frustrated by all the complaining we were doing. I was frustrated by the staff's unhelpfulness, when we complained. This was not how things were supposed to work. It was not supposed to be this hard. Despite our in-person protestations, nothing seemed to change or get better. No one seemed to care.

Beyond complaining to the staff at the center, it seemed like there was not much else we could do. And to everyone's credit, I think that that is a natural assumption—complain to the people who are actually at the center and doing the work. The problem was that that approach was not working. We needed another strategy.

As I struggled with the upset voices that surrounded me at the table, I just kept thinking, *"There has to be something we can do. What haven't we tried?"*

In my frustration, I opened up the Twitter app on my phone, thinking, *"Maybe I can tweet out something about this situation and that will get someone's attention?"*

Now keep in mind, this was happening in 2010—almost *10 years ago* and just 5 years after the platform started up. Twitter is now infamous for fielding angry customer service rants, but back then, it was not. In fact, back then, not many people were even familiar with the platform. It is estimated that in 2010, just over 50 million people were using Twitter.[1] While that may sound like a lot, that is just a drop in the bucket compared to the more than 320 million users that Twitter has today.

Moreover, at the time, no one else in my family was on Twitter—so no one else was familiar with the platform and how it might be used in a situation like this one. And they all thought the idea was crazy. The idea that I could post something called a "tweet" on a platform that not many people used and expect a helpful response—especially about an elderly woman's hospice care experience—seemed ridiculous.

But what did we have to lose? It was worth a shot, right? So I tweeted.

And to my—and everyone else's—surprise and excitement, a number of amazing things happened when I did.

First, even before I sent the tweet, I found that the hospice care center had a profile on Twitter so I could tag them in my message. (Who would have thought that a hospice center in New Jersey in 2010 would have a Twitter profile?)

Also, to my surprise, the center tweeted back immediately. The center's reply provided us with the phone number of a senior person at the center that we could call and talk to about what had been going on with my grandmother.

Then, when I called, the person I spoke with knew me by my tweet and was expecting my call.

The center had been monitoring tweets in real time, responding quickly to ones that were addressed to them with helpful information. They also alerted the right people at the center about the issue so that those people would expect the follow up call. Even today, this superior customer service would be a bit surprising (we would all like to hope that things will go this smoothly but we all know it does not always work out this way). But this was also almost 10 years ago—and they still got it right. Needless to say, my mind was blown.

That experience was life changing, both literally and figuratively. For me, this event illustrated the power of these new social media tools. It did not require that I be an "important person" to get help. It did not require a large Twitter following to have my issue addressed. I was an everyday person whose issue was just as important as anyone else's in that moment.

More importantly, however, it meant that for my grandmother, her quality of care improved. The person we spoke with was truly determined to help us get help for her and made sure she had all the proper care and services throughout the remainder of her time in hospice. And, indeed, she did not have any other issues while in their care. This allowed her to live out her last days with the grace and dignity she deserved.

And all of that was initiated through a little platform called Twitter.

At the time, I had been working in the field of social and digital media for a couple of years (mostly focused on social and digital media to promote health and behavior change) and these new and emerging social media platforms were just that—new and emerging. Twitter had just launched. Facebook had not launched its Pages feature yet. Instagram did not even exist.

Everyone who worked in this space—regardless of the topic they focused on—was just trying to figure this new world out. How to use these platforms? What to talk about? Who else was on these platforms with whom we could connect? And would this really take off? Should we be investing our time and effort into these platforms? Were people really going to see these platforms as a useful way to spend their time? Now these questions may seem naïve, but at the time, these were the issues that plagued us.

Regardless of these concerns, this experience with my grandma signaled something for me, something that I had not realized previously. The power of interpersonal connection—when fueled by technology—was going to have an enormous impact on health and behavior.

Moreover, this experience crystalized for me the kind of work I wanted to do—using these social and digital media tools to impact people's health for the better. And this aim has carried through to today. Since then, I have been working to understand and use social and digital media to support, expand, and improve the health of people globally.

But of course, everything changes. And social media is no different. Since my experience with the hospice care center on Twitter, the world of social media has been through a lot of shifts.

First, we have seen new platforms like Snapchat and Instagram enter the marketplace. There are also many more users of these platforms and, as a result, more content is being posted and taking up real estate across them.[2]

There has also been a change in the type of content that is given prominence on these social media platforms, shifting, generally speaking, from unpaid to paid content. This trend has been happening since 2014, and if you have managed a Facebook Business Page over the past several years, you've likely noticed a drop in the reach of your content when not supported with advertising dollars.

This is also affecting how users interact with these platforms and what content they are seeing. This growth in paid content has also lead to the use of ad blockers. Ad blockers, or ad filtering as it also referred to, is the use of different types of software to remove or alter online advertising in a web browser or mobile application.[3] More and more social media users are using these—both on their mobile devices as well as on desktop devices—to avoid seeing paid ads. Some of the latest data suggest that *nearly* 70% of 18- to 24-year olds use ad blockers.[4] This means that while paid content is often given priority in terms of visibility in social media, even social media ads are not reaching a large swath of consumers.

Taken together, these changes and barriers make it increasingly hard for communicators and marketers to get their message out. If organic content is not being seen and ads are being blocked, what options are left?

Well, in the last couple of years, we have seen the rise of the "online influencer." Online influencers, generally speaking, are everyday people who are incredibly influential within their online social networks. What makes them so unique however is the medium in which they operate and wield this influence. While you could argue that lots of everyday people are influential to us—that friend in yoga, another mom at your child's school, a professional contact—these online opinion leaders are especially influential because they have established online profiles, talk about a topic or set of topics they are familiar with, and have a cohort of followers who trust their thoughts, opinions, and perspectives.

What makes this world of online influencers so powerful is the fact that these online opinion leaders have engaged (and often large) followings, which leads to high engagement with their posts, which, in turn, drives increased visibility of content. They, therefore, have the ability to help promote content that otherwise would not be seen. In this way, they can act as an antidote to the challenges that marketers are otherwise facing.

And because of this, the use of these influencers is becoming increasingly popular with marketers, public relations professionals, and communicators across the globe.[5] Moreover, online influencers are getting paid to share their thoughts, opinions, and perspectives. In fact, paid influencer marketing—or the act of paying online influencers to endorse messages and products and which is often identified by disclosure language on a blog by the #ad or #sponsored hashtag in a post—grew by nearly 200 percent in 2017 and had a reach of more than 1.5 million worldwide.[6]

So it is within this context that I found my work shifting—very organically—to working with influencers to support health programs and initiatives. And I have been doing this kind of work for over a decade now.

My work with influencers began back in 2006—back before they were actually called "influencers." At the time, I worked in what was called "organic marketing." These were the early days of what would eventually become known as "influencer marketing" and the juvenescence of the industry meant a few things—few best practices about working with influences existed; networks of influencers were still very much in their infancy; and while payment for posts certainly existed back then, it was not the driving force in the industry that it is today.

Despite this—or maybe because of it—during this time, we ran some of the most interesting campaigns of the day. We worked with YouTube creators on behalf our client, GEICO, to integrate the company's mascot, the gecko, into the top performing videos of the day.[7] We also ran some of the first new product launch campaigns with influencers for brands such as Horizon Organic and Silk Soymilk.

But after 2 years of working in the private sector, I wanted to get back into issue-related work. So I returned to the public health world to take what I knew and apply it to a whole different set of initiatives.

Upon returning to public health, one of the first campaigns I ran was a Tweet-a-Thon to support adolescent vaccination. A first for a public health initiative, we worked with a network that was, at the time, called TwitterMoms (now they are called SocialMoms), to engage moms on Twitter to talk with their followers about adolescent vaccination recommendations.

Since then, I have led numerous campaigns that have utilized everyday influencers to support and promote some of the most challenging and stigmatized health issues of our time, e.g., seasonal flu vaccination, adolescent, specifically Human Papillomavirus (HPV), vaccination, back-to-school efforts, birth defects prevention, early hearing loss, Zika awareness and prevention, sickle cell disease awareness, and HIV testing.

During this same time, I decided to go back to school to get my PhD, focusing my dissertation research on online influencers as opinion leaders for health information dissemination. Over the course of my doctoral program and my professional work, which happened simultaneously, I have been able to conduct research and run campaigns with hundreds of influencers. This work has leveraged influencers to both disseminate health messages and understand the effects that influencer engagement in health programs can have on their followers and beyond. This has given me a unique perspective on the culture of this influencer world, how it has shifted over time, the struggles that influencers face as social and digital media moves forward as an industry, and the opportunities for health promotion and improving lives that these influencers have the ability to bring about.

Perhaps most importantly, though: my time spent working on this topic has taken me to places I never thought I'd go. I have had the opportunity to meet and speak with numerous influencers about their work and the role of health in their work. I have been moved to tears upon hearing about some of their personal struggles with health issues and the impact that those experiences have had on them and their writing. I have also been given hope because of their commitment to "make a difference" in their own lives, within their families, and in their communities.

I want to share these stories with you. I want you to see them as I do and to be moved as I have been.

I also want to share the larger story of influencers and health with you in the hopes that this story will motivate experts from both the health and influencer worlds to seek each other out and work together to make our world a better place. Just as it is important to share evidence-based information with people, it is also important to have that information shared via trusted sources in a voice and tone that speaks to the everyday person.

I am motivated to do this because, quite frankly, we are a sick country. According to America's Health Rankings, in the past 3 years, deaths from drug overdoses have increased 25% and the rate of obesity among adults has increased by 5%.[8] As well, mental distress is also on the rise, with rates among adults increasing by 7% in the last 2 years.

Yet, despite these statistics, which are staggering, I have hope. These influencers inspire me every day. I am excited by the work they are motivated to do on their own to bring awareness to important health issues. I am also excited by the work that I get to do with them on these topics. They make me excited for a future of health where experts in the health and digital fields are working together to improve lives.

About this book

This is why I wrote this book. To share their stories and some of what I know. And hopefully inspire a new set of marketers and communicators to pursue this kind of work and make a difference in this world.

So I am supposed to tell you what to expect (and what not to expect) from this book. Well, here is a taste.

What this book is NOT.
Sometimes it is easier to start with what something is not. I know exactly what this book is not. And why no other writer could write this exact book.

It is not academic. Yes, I have a PhD. And yes, much of this book is based on my own research and work. However, I did not want this book to end up stuck on a shelf—or in a lofty ivory tower somewhere—that no one would read and no one would find useful. I did not want this to be written in a language that only academics could understand. I did not want this to be alienating to the everyday person who may work in this area (or may be interested in working in this area).

It is not a blog post on data. I am not going to promise you a book on the latest and greatest social media data—that will, in fact, get old really quickly. I reference data throughout the book, but this is not meant to be a state of social media and influencer marketing in 2019.

It is not about celebrity. Celebrity endorsers have been around for a long time, and the advent of the Internet has resulted in the explosion of brand- and product-related endorsements by celebrities. I will reference celebrity influencers throughout this book, but this book is not about celebrities.

It is not a one-size-fits-all 'how-to' book. I am also not going to give you a one-size-fits-all approach to working with influencers. There really is not just one approach, and you should stop reading right now if you just want a "how-to" book. There are plenty of other books out there that can help you with that.

What this book IS.

So if we know that this book is not, then we can start to tease apart what it is.

It is based on data. This book is, first and foremost, based on data. It draws from my own research and work in this area. It includes data that I collected for my dissertation research surveying and interviewing hundreds of influencers over the course of a year. My research considered various characteristics of these influencers including their gender, age, geographical location, race/ethnicity, and theme or topic of their blog and social media profiles, e.g., travel, health, and parenting. Therefore, throughout this book, I describe the influencers I interviewed using some of these characteristics. This is to give you a picture of who they are and what they are all about. These descriptors help provide perspective and depth to the comments and feedback I share throughout the following chapters. This book also draws from the latest industry data.

It is grounded in theory. This book is also based on theory. It draws from prior research with bloggers and online influencers, but it also goes beyond the online space to draw on the knowledgebase about opinion leaders more generally and the roles they play in improving health and people's lives. It draws from theories about social networks and interpersonal relationships—and it touches on the constructs of credibility, trust, and willingness to communicate about health issues. It also discusses influencers' perceptions of risk and prevention as they relate to health and how these perceptions manifest in terms of the content that influencers want to share on their blogs and social media and the topics they are willing to write about. This is all done in order to build a case that online influencers are modern-day opinion leaders—and that for health, this is very powerful.

It is my personal perspective on the topic. While you will get data and theory in this book, you will also get my own personal perspectives and learnings from the research and projects that I am working on or have worked on. Throughout the book, I am going to share relevant stories from everyday influencers—some of whom you may be familiar with already and others who may be new to you. While I would like to believe that I am completely objective, I know I am not, and as such, this book is imbued with my personal thoughts, perspectives, and biases about the topic.

It is a mix of private sector and health-related applications. But really, it's mostly about health. Influencers have emerged as powerful voices online because of the brands that have been willing to engage them. As I noted above, some of my earliest work with influencers was in support of brand campaigns, so stories from that time will help provide a backdrop as we assess the role of online influencers in information dissemination, promotion, and engagement. However, most of my work with influencers has been focused on health topics, so much of the book will draw heavily from this experience.

It is about everyday people. I mentioned earlier that this book is not about celebrity influencers. Rather, it is about everyday people who are influential within their social networks—those everyday opinion leaders who talk about their kids, or the new local news, or the new SoulCycle that opened up by them, or the weather, or their latest vacation. These are people like you and me. They are your mom, your dad, your sister or your brother. They are your best friend or your favorite co-worker. They have a voice and an audience that listens to that voice. And that voice and audience are amplified through the use of social media technology. Because of this, they are uniquely positioned to weave health messages into everyday content and conversations—and thereby, make the health conversation relevant to all sorts of *other* everyday people.

It is about contextualizing conversations about health within everyday conversations. One thing you might expect in a book about influencers and health is that I am going to primarily talk about health blogs and websites. Well, that is not what this book is about. Nope. Not going to do it. Not at all.

As I already mentioned, what I am actually most interested in is how we integrate health into everyday conversations and tie health to things that people love and do—*naturally.*

Let us be honest, for MOST of us, we do not love doing the things that are the best for us. While I love fresh fruits and vegetables, I also love snacks and sweets. While I love running and yoga, I also love to be a couch potato. We're human. We do not think about health all day, every day, and that is okay. But that is exactly why, as health communicators and marketers, we also need to find ways to have the important conversations when they matter in ways that make sense and are relevant to people. Because of this, most of my work revolves around finding ways to integrate health messages into other non–health-specific contexts.

It is for both marketers and communicators as well as influencers. This book is, first and foremost, written about what I have learned through my work with influencers. Because of this, it has direct application for marketers, communicators, organizations, and businesses seeking to understand this space and how to engage in it.

However, as noted above, weaving health messages into everyday conversations is not necessarily something we are all familiar with or comfortable doing. And it has been my experience that often influencers themselves do not initially see how health can fit into their blog or social media content—unless they already write about health. Therefore, connecting the dots between the different topics influencers write about and how health might fit in is another aim of this book and something that influencers themselves might find interesting.

It is geared to U.S. audiences—but has application for broader, international audiences. Health issues are most often endemic to the places where we live. While we are a global community, each country faces unique health challenges that other countries may not face. In the United States, we face issues such as obesity and anti-vaccine-related outbreaks. In other counties, communicable diseases, such as malaria, tuberculosis, and diarrheal diseases, are the major causes of morbidity and mortality. Many of the topics I discuss in this book are U.S.-specific, but I do touch on ones that effect other countries as well.

While Internet usage and penetration is on the rise—it is estimated that there are currently more than 2 billion social media users globally[9]—different countries may have unique use patterns and platform preferences. And of course, any conversation about online influencers will have to take into account a particular community's level of Internet access in order for that conversation to be relevant. However, online influencers face fewer barriers of time and space. Their messages can be easily seen by anyone with a mobile device and a connection to the Internet. Therefore, online influencers, while very popular in the United States, are also influential worldwide.

It also just so happens that most of my work with influencers has been focused on U.S.-based influencers, campaigns, and health issues. Therefore, these make up the majority of the examples I write about in this book.

Thus, there is the potential that the contents of this book may be more relevant to U.S.-based marketers, health communicators, and influencers. Having said that, there may still be lessons that anyone anywhere in the world can take away from it.

A few notes about the content.

As noted above, for the purpose of this book, I define influencer as "an everyday layperson endorser."

The personal stories that I reference throughout this book have been anonymized by removing names and specific identifying details about the influencers. This has been done to protect their identities. This is a normal research practice. I also have the consent of these influencers to share their stories.

Quotes included here are taken from the interviews I have conducted, the responses I received to the open-ended questions in my survey, my personal conversations with influencers and other experts in the field, and interviews with experts or well-known influencers that have been published elsewhere. Unless referencing someone well-known, these are also anonymized.

I do provide tips and advice on working with influencers, but what this book gives you is more of a peek inside a community that is self-generated, motivated, changing quickly, finding its identity in a fast-paced world, and learning more and more about itself every day.

Finally, I can only say that I stand on the shoulders of giants—this book builds on the great work of so many great researchers, data scientists, influencers, storytellers, communicators, and health promoters that have come before me. I am thankful for them and hope that others continue to build on this work into the future.

How you should read—and use—this book. My intention with this book is to give you a sense of how to engage influencers in your work, especially if you work in health. However, I also hope that this book is not something that you read once and just put back on the shelf (digital or otherwise).

No matter what industry you are in, I think there is something you can take away from this book. And I hope you do. As you read it, think about how to bring the tips and advice I include here into other relevant conversations you may have at work and at home. I hope you use this information to have better conversations with influencers, to make the case at work for why this area is important, and that you use the lessons I have learned, and share here, to successfully integrate influencer marketing into the work you do.

I also hope it ultimately results in fruitful collaborations that advance healthy outcomes.

Final Reflections

So if you have made it this far and I have piqued your interest, I'm happy. And I hope you decide to read further. What follows is a bit of history about opinion leaders and how today's influencers act as modern-day versions of these, especially as it applies to the health context. Additionally, I review the importance of relationships to the business-side of the industry, including how the industry is changing and therefore how those relationships are also changing. I review influencers' thoughts about communicating about health and their perceptions of risk and fatalism. Finally, I discuss their thoughts on messaging and creative preferences.

As you venture into the subsequent chapters of this book, I will accompany you along this journey. But let me share some final words with you here. We all have probably seen or experienced some of the best things that social media have to offer. Maybe you have reconnected with long lost friends or family. Maybe you have found a new job. Maybe you heard a new song or got inspired to take a trip somewhere you have never been.

Or maybe you know someone who, by posting a picture on social media and allowing their community to comment on it, was able to take action and prevent or treat a health issue he/she didn't even know he/she had. Maybe that person was you.

Does any of this sound familiar? Yes? Well, these are the great things that can happen in social media. These are the success stories.

But we have also seen some really ugly things happen in and because of social media. Things like bullying, inappropriate use of people's data, fake profiles, and fake news.

While these things may taint the medium, it is not just about "good" or "bad" use cases. It is about responsibility.

Ultimately, it is a *responsibility* to use social media. It is a *responsibility* to be an influencer and to work with online influencers. It is a *responsibility* you have to yourself, to your followers, to your family and to your friends, and to your community. And everyone has to own that responsibility to make it work.

Hopefully this book provides you with an understanding of the world of influencers; inspiration to make you want to engage in this space to better yourself, your families, your communities, and our world; the tools and frameworks to do so successfully; and the caution to do so ethically.

Thank you for taking a chance on this book. I hope it inspires you the way I have been inspired.

Chapter 1

Influencers: Old and New

in·flu·encer | /ˈinflo͝oənsər/ | noun
A person or thing that influences another.

Mad Cow Disease is one of the most salient public health crises that I can recall from my childhood that *did not* happen in the United States.

In case you are not familiar with Mad Cow Disease, it is a fatal condition that affects the brain and nervous system in animals and can be passed to humans who have eaten infected meat.

The outbreak that happened in the 1990s—the one that garnered all the media attention—actually started in Britain; and while it would eventually show up in the United States in the early 2000s, during the media frenzy the 1990s, there were, in fact, no cases of Mad Cow in the United States.[10]

Despite being a non–red meat eater myself, and despite there being no cases of infection in the United States at the time, I remember the Mad Cow Disease outbreak of the 1990s as being terrifying. I think this was in part because I was not really aware of outbreaks before then but also because I felt like it was being talked about *everywhere*—all over the media and in everyday conversations.

If you do not remember the outbreak itself, you may remember something that happened as a result of it. In 1996, during the outbreak, as the controversial practices within the beef industry were beginning to come to light within the media and among the general public, Oprah Winfrey featured the story on her show, interviewing rancher-turned-animal-rights activist, Howard Lyman.[11]

During the interview, as Lyman talked about the subpar practices in the beef industry that were causing these public safety issues, Oprah exclaimed that such revelations had "stopped [her] cold from eating another hamburger!"

In response to this comment, beef prices plunged. And they would continue to do so, eventually reaching a 10-year low.

Thus, it appeared that with a single statement—one, of course, that was shared with millions of viewers—Oprah managed to sway millions of Americans' willingness to eat meat.

But was she really able to sway popular opinion so quickly? Was it just a coincidence that Oprah made her comment and then beef prices plummeted? Or was there something bigger going on here?

At the time, many people thought that this decreased consumption of meat by American consumers could be directly attributed to Oprah's hamburger comment. So much so in fact, that in response to Oprah's comment and the apparent impact it had on the beef industry, a group of cattle ranchers in Texas filed a $10.3 million lawsuit against the talk show host claiming that her statement defamed the entire industry, caused the drop in price, and hurt their business.

What these angry cattle ranchers had identified vis-à-vis their lawsuit—whether they knew it or not at the time—was what has become known as "the Oprah effect."[12] "The Oprah effect" refers to Oprah Winfrey's ability to sway the opinions of millions of consumers about a subject, item, or person that she features on one of her many media platforms. And most often, "the effect" has resulted in positive outcomes for the subject, item, or person that is featured.

For instance, in 2015, "the Oprah effect" went into overdrive sending stock prices soaring when Oprah announced that she had acquired 10 percent of Weight Watchers stock. She has also helped launch the careers of numerous people including psychologist, Dr. Phil, health expert, Dr. Oz, alternative-medicine advocate, Deepak Chopra, financial adviser, Suze Orman, and lifestyle designer, Nate Berkus—all of whom have been featured on her show or across her other media platforms. Over the years, she has also single-handedly popularized numerous books, magazines, movies, television, fashion and lifestyle products, and political causes.

But the "effect" has also worked the other way—turning consumers off of something. This was the case with beef during the Mad Cow Disease outbreak. It was also the case for author Jonathan Franzen. In 2001, Oprah picked a Jonathan Franzen's book for her book club and invited the author on her show. In response, he suggested that going on television to promote a book would lessen his standing in what he called, "the high-art literary tradition." Oprah responded by rescinding her invitation, and as a result, many people, including those in the "high-art literary tradition," rebuked the author.

All of these "Oprah effect" examples reveal how it only takes one person to have an impact on the opinions and perspectives of other people. In the case of Mad Cow Disease, it only required one highly influential person sharing a personal opinion about a topic that was top-of-mind for consumers to sway public opinion. And that ability to influence opinions so swiftly had substantial consequences.

Being influential about books or products, or even Mad Cow disease, does not necessarily equate though to being influential about all topics. And it certainly does not mean that you are influential when it comes to health. Health is very personal. Health is sensitive. Health is private. Health can also be highly stigmatized. So how does "the Oprah effect" translate into the health context more broadly?

Well, right around the same time that the Mad Cow Disease outbreak was happening in Britain, across the globe, Thailand was dealing with an outbreak of its own. Only, this one was an outbreak of HIV infections.[13]

Now Thailand has historically been a leader in the fight against HIV/AIDS. The country recorded its first cases of HIV in 1984. However, by the early 1990s, HIV infections were spreading across the country like wildfire.

Moreover, while this outbreak was affecting Thailand's population as a whole, it was hitting certain subgroups harder than others. In particular, Thailand's sex worker population was being severely impacted. Data from that time suggest that between 1989 and 1990, the percentage of sex workers infected with HIV tripled from 3.1 to 9.3 percent. Then, *just a year later*, in 1991, it jumped again. This time to 15 percent.

Of course, any subgroup being hit so hard with an outbreak is not good, but when a subgroup like sex workers is impacted this hard, it means ripple effects. Big ripple effects. It was estimated at the time that the average sex worker had about 100 clients per year. This meant that for each infected sex worker, approximately 100 other individuals were being put at risk for an infection, and then, those people, who had other relationships, partners, and families, were potentially infecting a whole other cadre of people.

Given the increasing number of infections within the sex worker population, and the fact that this group was central to this epidemiological social network, addressing the issue directly with the sex workers population became vital to Thailand's ability to curb the outbreak.

It was with this acknowledgement that Thailand became the first country in Asia to publicly declare a serious HIV/AIDS problem and commit to dealing with the issue. And with that, they launched the 100 percent Condom Use Programme nationwide.

While Thailand's public recognition of the outbreak and promise of a solution was both novel and progressive, as many of us who work in the health industry know, launching a campaign does not guarantee that anything will change. And for the Thai government, working with the sex worker population would indeed prove to be challenging.

A main challenge the Thai government faced was the fact that the commercial sex industry in Thailand is illegal. This meant that acknowledging the issue and implementing policies to regulate it would be difficult.

Related to this, the government received resistance from the owners of commercial sex establishments. The owners feared that forcing their sex workers to use condoms would be economically damaging to their business. In short, unless *all* businesses agreed to requiring their sex workers to use condoms, owners expected to lose customers who could just choose to go to another establishment.

There were also logistical challenges to making condoms easily and widely available that the Thai government would have to tackle.

And finally, the government would come to learn that some of the biggest barriers they faced were from the sex workers themselves. First, the Thai government came to understand that sex workers' basic understanding about the benefits of condom use was limited. As well, they discovered that, oftentimes, sex workers did not possess the agency or negotiating skills required to be able to dissuade customers from wanting to have sex without a condom.

At the heart of all of these challenges was one central challenge—condom use was highly stigmatized within Thai culture. The 100 percent Condom Use Programme knew it was going to need strategies that addressed this stigma if anything was going to change.

Now, the concept of stigma is interesting because it is heavily related to communication. That is, if and how we talk about a health issue facilitates how we ultimately think about that issue.[14] For instance, communication (or lack thereof) can lead to the spread of misinformation or a lack of understanding about an issue. However, communication also can lead to the eradication of stigma as dialogue about a topic enables increased understanding. In fact, there is evidence that suggests that the influence of interpersonal communication can aid in addressing stigma.[15,16]

Therefore, and perhaps not surprisingly, a main strategy that the Thai government employed to address the challenges it faced was the use of opinion leaders who were highly influential in Thai culture. Specifically, the government engaged media spokespeople to include messages about HIV/AIDS and the importance of condom use in their television programs and shows, as well as Buddhist monks to bless condoms and sprinkle them with holy water.

These opinion leaders were selected because they were influential to many different types of people including sex workers and the general public. By involving these cultural opinion leaders, information about HIV was communicated to a large portion of the population by those they trusted and people could engage in a social dialogue about condom use.

And it worked! Creating such a social dialogue helped to reduce people's resistance to condom use, and by 1992, use of condoms in sex worker establishments had increased to more than 90 percent. Moreover, the World Bank estimated that this campaign prevented nearly 200,000 new cases of HIV/AIDS.

This story evinces how it was not enough for the Thai government to recognize that there was an issue with HIV infections in the country. It demonstrates that it was not enough for the government to create a campaign. It showcases how it was not enough to just tell people to wear condoms and expect that they would do so.

Rather, the government had to recognize the key barriers it faced in trying to change people's behavior. To overcome these, the government had to also find a way to start a dialogue about the issue. By leveraging influential voices, the government was able to jumpstart a social conversation that eventually reduced stigma, normalized the behavior, and saved lives.

Opinion leaders can come in many different shapes and sizes. The examples of Oprah and Thailand demonstrate this. Both of these stories also showcase how substantially opinions can be swayed by engaging people who are influential to the communities they reach.

At this point, you may be wondering why we are talking about Oprah and Buddhist monks when this book is supposed to be about online influencers. Well, in order to understand the world of online influencers, we must first talk about opinion leaders. And to do this, we must go back to the very beginning. This will be the focus of the rest of this chapter.

A Brief History of Opinion Leadership

The two stories this chapter opened with exemplify how influencers can change people's behaviors—whether intentionally (as seen in the Thailand example) or unintentionally (as seen in the Oprah example).

But to talk about influencers does not always mean talking about celebrities or prominent spokespeople. It also means talking about the everyday people who inform our decisions, our choices, and our lives—whether we know it or not. And to talk about people who are influential to us is to talk about opinion leadership.

Opinion leadership is based on the premise that most people form their opinions under the influence of others whom they hold in high esteem.[17] These could be people we do not know personally but know of due to their level of fame or position within a community. The media celebrities and spokespeople and the Buddhist monks (from the earlier stories) are examples of this type. They could also be people we know well like friends, family, teachers, or neighbors.

The concept of opinion leadership is a part of the theory of the diffusion of innovations (DOI), which refers to the spread of new ideas, or innovations, through different channels over time throughout a social system, e.g., a group of individuals or an organization.[18] DOI has been studied as far back as the 19th century,[19] and while there have been many researchers who have examined DOI, perhaps no one is more strongly associated with the concept than Everett M. Rogers.

Rogers suggests that there are five categories of adopters: the innovators (who are the first in a social system to try out something new), the early adopters, the early majority, the late majority, and finally, the laggards (who are the last group to try out the innovation). However, the diffusion process can be dynamic, rather than linear; and this is due in part to numerous actors within a network who play important, but different, roles in the process of spreading an innovation throughout that network.

Opinion leaders are one of these actor types, and they can appear in any of these adoption categories. They tend not to be the innovators of the group because they are not necessarily the first to try something new, and they are not the laggards because they influence others to adopt this new thing. Rather, they lie somewhere between the innovators and the laggards.

Opinion leaders are powerful because they both act as sources for new ideas for others, and they have the ability to identify and convince others to adopt these new ideas.[20] They have this ability because they often are similar to those they influence, and their influence tends to remain steady over time.[21] In fact, opinion leaders can actually jumpstart the spread and adoption of new behaviors because of their influence.[22]

Why Opinion Leaders Are Important

Opinion leaders are said to play several critical roles in the introduction of new ideas. For health, these roles are critical to the implementation of various programs and interventions.

The primary role opinion leaders play is to provide "entrée and legitimation to external change agents."[23] These "external change agents" may be anyone or any entity seeking to introduce new ideas, information, or behaviors into a group of people. That is to say that because they are already a member of or associated with a community, they have established trust with the members of that community. And that familiarity and trust allows them to successfully introduce new people and new ideas to that community.

They can also be the actual communicators of a particular message to their community and provide a channel for communication back to the external change agents. Opinion leaders may often act as primary communicators or negotiators between a community and the "outsiders" who are trying to engage with that community. They can help communicate new ideas to a community in a manner that can result in these ideas being positively accepted, as was seen with the Buddhist monks in the story about Thailand. They can also share community concerns back with these "outsiders." This communication role is vital in helping bridge differences between the groups and overcoming barriers to change.

Third, they can act as "role models for behavior change within the community." Often, opinion leaders may be able to demonstrate firsthand that a new idea or behavior is valuable and will not have ill effects on the members of the community. They can do this by modeling that behavior first for the rest of their community.

Finally, they may act as "the capital" that is left behind in the community after the external change agent has left. This can help institutionalize ideas and behaviors. As noted earlier, opinion leaders are trusted members of their communities.

That trust comes from the fact that they have been affiliated with that community long before the external change agent came along wanting to introduce a new idea to its members, and they will remain affiliated long after that external change agent has left. Such a steadfast role is what makes them opinion leaders for that community and helps ensure that the new idea can continue to exist and propagate in the community long after the external change agent has departed. In short, their presence gives these interventions permanence and longevity.

Opinion Leaders in the Age of the Internet

While the concept of opinion leaders is not new, the advent of the Internet has opened up channels of communication—and possible influence—that are new.

Seventy percent of Americans now use social media to connect with one another, engage with news content, and share information.[24] Thus, individuals from all walks of life can now have access to more information, access it more quickly, and have it curated through the online channels they trust. Moreover, as more and more people participate in virtual communities and social media to connect and communicate with others like them, the opportunity for the development of online opinion leaders is growing.[25]

Blogs and social media platforms such as Twitter, Facebook, Instagram, Snapchat, and YouTube represent some of these flourishing online communities where many varied interpersonal interactions take place.

Moreover, the ecosystem for these online opinion leaders is extensive. It goes beyond blogs and your traditional social media platforms to also encompass private online groups such as those found on Facebook, private communities such as those that can be found on the platform, NING, groups on the popular platform, Reddit (otherwise known as "sub-Reddits"), and even podcasts.

Across these different platforms and media, different types of information are shared by their users. This social media activity generates a massive amount of text-based, photo, audio, and video content.[26] Moreover, the speed and scale at which this information is shared online is unprecedented.

More specifically, however, this activity generates a plethora of comments and discussion between these users and their followers. And opinions and ideas are shared as part of these online discussions. Thus, bloggers, social media users, and private community members have a virtual "finger on the pulse" of the needs and beliefs of their online audiences and can act as modern-day online opinion leaders for them.

"Online Influencers" Are Today's Modern Opinion Leaders

Thus far, we have discussed the broad concept of opinion leaders and how today, these have migrated online to become a modern-day version of this age-old concept.

Today, we refer to these online opinion leaders as "online influencers"—and there are a couple of different types of them.

Celebrity influencers are perhaps the most well-known online influencer type. We already saw in the stories about Oprah and Thailand how media and celebrity spokespeople can act as influencers. And today, you cannot open your Instagram app or watch a video online without seeing some sort of celebrity-endorsed product advertisement. From Selena Gomez to Kim Kardashian to Lebron James to Kevin Hart, celebrities seem to be everywhere online endorsing product after product.

There is a long history of using celebrities to successfully change consumer attitudes and opinions.[27] Celebrity figures are often perceived as competent, trustworthy, and credible, with these attributes positively affecting audiences' perceptions of advertising.[28–30]

However, celebrities are not the only ones doing the influencing. There are also what I refer to as blog-turned-publishing-house influencers. Yes, that is a long title. But it really does sum up who they are and where they fit in this space. This type refers to influencers who have leveraged their online profile to create a new type of presence—one that is focused on what is called "word-of-mouth publishing." This has resulted from years of posting their thoughts online and building up a following. They, then, parley their perspectives and attentive audiences into the creation of a website that is run more like a publishing house with large teams that help run it, develop content, and engage with brands and campaigns. Examples of this influencer type include Jill Smokler of Scary Mommy and Amy Morrison of Pregnant Chicken.

Finally, there are everyday layperson influencers. And these can take many different forms. For instance, they include bloggers, Instagrammers, and Twitter and Facebook users. Even video content platforms like YouTube are also spawning their own form of layperson influencers.[31]

Some of these have reached such notariety that they are called "insta-celebrities.[32]

The main appeal of everyday layperson influencers is that they are ordinary people giving an ordinary person's perspective. They talk about a range of subjects, from gaming and fashion to music and politics. Their "ordinariness" and their accessibility allow their audiences to identify with them. This leads to a higher than normal level of notoriety for an everyday person, and with that popularity, some have become incredibly powerful as they are able to influence the opinions and purchasing behaviors of huge numbers of people.[33]

Final Reflections

Whether intentional or unintentional, whether online or offline, opinion leaders are incredibly influential with the communities they serve. Oprah allegedly impacted an entire industry with just one statement. The Thai government knew that to change people's behaviors and curb an epidemic, cultural opinion leaders would need to be a part of the conversation. Their words alone were not going to be enough; people needed to hear about it from others they trusted.

Today, opinion leadership happens online through many varied channels and many different types of influencers. These influencers understand consumer opinions *and* that they have the ability to sway them.

But what does it take to do this? We learned earlier that opinion leaders are influential because they tend to be similar to the people they influence. But what is really going on in those relationships? Specifically, what is it about the relationship between influencers and their followers that contributes to this influence? And what does it actually take to be considered an online influencer? We will explore these things in the next chapter.

Chapter 2

Understanding the Relationship between Influencers and Their Followers

fol·low·er | /ˈfälōər/ | noun
One that follows the opinions or teachings of another.

While influencer marketing is a concept that has more recently become popularized, online influencers are not new. In fact, they have been around for decades now. We just did not always call them "online influencers."

One of the first people ever to start a blog—and "make it big" blogging—was Heather Armstrong. Armstrong is the Salt Lake City-based creator of the blog, *Dooce*. Considered to be one of the first mommy bloggers—*ever*—she started blogging nearly 20 years ago in 2001.

While she is now well-known as a mommy blogger, at the time when she started her blog, she was not a mom or even married. She was single—so she wrote about single-woman things, e.g., pop culture, music, and her own life experiences.[34]

And it is with this set of topics that she began her journey to becoming one of the most popular bloggers out there.

She did not remain single, though. Over time, she went on to get married, have children, and go through a whole host of new life experiences. And as a result, her blog content also changed. So as she went through these different experiences and shared them on her blog, her writing chronicled her journey from single woman to wife to mother.

But when she started her blog back in 2001, she never thought that anyone would ever read it.[35] Very quickly, however, she would amass such a large following that she would be able to parlay her blog into a business that could financially support her entire family.[36] You might recall that we discussed in Chapter 1 that there are these blog-turned-publishing-house type influencers. Well, Heather Armstrong is another example of these word-of-mouth publishing influencers.

And just 4 years later, by 2005, she was working full time on the site. Her husband worked with her, and she had an assistant who also supported work on the blog. Collectively, these efforts generated 100,000 daily readers as well as hundreds of thousands of dollars in advertising revenue.

Incredible, right? It is. Armstrong's popularity and success is indeed impressive. But, it begs the question, what has made her *so* well liked by her readers?

Well, Armstrong's style of writing is one of the things that is often referred to when talking about her appeal with her followers. She has always written her blog content with humor and honesty. For instance, she has written about her husband changing a poopy diaper after giving their first-born child refried beans. She has also written about "real people" moments like the time when she dropped her kids off at school with "[her] face still imprinted with the outline of [her] pillow [and her] hair a nest of unruly tangles."[37] Her stories are ones that many people, especially parents, can relate to.

This style of writing drew readers in initially and it keeps them coming back for more. In fact, it is her sense of humor and her honest and transparent writing about her personal and parenting life that she became known for early on.

However, I would argue that it is also the variety of topics that she tackles on her blog that makes her appealing. From the seemingly mundane everyday issues that she writes about to more serious topics that others might shy away from, readers can continuously return to her blog (or listen to her podcast now-a-days) for both humorous takes on poop and braces (not necessarily together) and really honest writing about the things she is struggling with.

For example, one of the most personal and private topics she ever talked about was her struggle with depression and anxiety after the birth of her first daughter. During this time, she wrote candidly about spending months getting psychiatric and medical treatment for her depression and anxiety—only to have her anxiety worsen over that time period. She also wrote about the many different types of medications she tried (e.g., Risperdal, Ativan, Trazadone, Lamictal, Effexor, Abilify, Strattera, Klonopin, Seroquel),[38] and how none of them seemed to work for her. Finally, she wrote about how, when those things did not work—and she still did not feel better, as she put it—she checked herself into a psychiatric ward.[39]

Perhaps, most poignantly, she wrote about wanting to hurt herself and the stigma of mental health issues, stating,

> When people say that they cannot believe I'm being so open about this I want to ask them WHY NOT? Why should there be any shame in getting help for a disease? If there is a stigma to this, let there be one. At least I am alive. At least my baby still has her mother. At least I have a chance at a better life.

As well, she wrote,

> And I guess I'm trying to understand why anyone would resist trying to work through an issue that is making their life miserable, and that maybe if I came

> out and talked about what I have been through and how I feel about what I've been through, that someone may feel a little less embarrassed about getting help.

Moreover, the issues she writes about and the way she tells her stories connects with people on a personal level. They make her and her readers feel like they are not alone. They create a sense of community as people recognize and relate to each other's experiences. So you can laugh and cry and get mad along with her as she tells you her stories. You can relate to the situations she finds herself in because it is likely that you have been there before yourself.

For instance, when she was talking about her mental health issues, she wrote,

> I have found solace in the stories you have sent to me, comfort in knowing that I am not alone in this struggle. I may not be able to see your faces, but I can hear your voices.

So it would seem that there is not a topic that Armstrong will not tackle.

But that's not exactly true. There would come a time, in fact, when she would go through something that was deeply personal and decide to limit how much she shared about it. And when this happened, her reputation for honest and transparent writing would ultimately create a whole new set of challenges for Armstrong.

That time came in 2012 when Armstrong and her husband announced that they were divorcing.

During the course of their divorce, beyond sharing the initial news that she was separating from her husband, she wrote that she would not be sharing more details about her divorce on her blog. For her, the experience of divorce was more complex than, say, her struggles with depression, because it involved people other than herself. Sharing her personal struggles with depression felt okay to her because she was telling her own story from her own perspective, but divorce has many sides, and many people who are affected by it. Therefore, sharing this experience only from her perspective would be biased and unfair.

Unfortunately, her choice not to share caused some of her readers to become upset. And when Armstrong decided to pause her blog altogether, she drew even more ire. She announced this decision to pause her blog in a post, entitled "*Looking upward and ahead*," to which one reader responded,

> This is the hugest betrayal, we've invested our time in you when we could have been following other bloggers, you owe it to us to continue. How dare you take your children away from us!

Thus, it is clear how Armstrong's authentic and humorous way of storytelling resulted in the creation of a loyal group of followers who connected to her through the stories she shared about her life. However, this connection she established also meant that they reacted strongly when those personal tidbits were taken away. In fact, when asked about her relationship with her readers and how the decision not to share certain information caused such a backlash, she acknowledged how complex the relationship between a blogger and her readers can be, stating,

> Something of a contentious relationship can develop between bloggers and our readers. We've invited readers into our lives. But, it's always been the case that we're not showing them everything and when that becomes clearer at certain times, they get angry. A lot of readers wanted to know every single detail of my divorce and when I refused to satisfy that desire they got really angry. Just because I've made a living telling stories about myself, doesn't mean I owe you my life.

These feelings of disappointment, however, are probably ones we can all relate to. Recall for a moment how you felt when *The Sopranos* ended. Or *Sex and the City*. Or *Breaking Bad*.

Or even more recently *Game of Thrones*. Or how you felt when your favorite pair of shoes was discontinued. Or your favorite bookstore closed. Losing access to a beloved product even made it into an episode of *Seinfeld*. You might remember the episode where Elaine learned that her contraceptive of choice was being discontinued, so she bought one of the last cases of sponges and scrutinized each of her dates for their "sponge-worthiness" in order to maximize the length of time she could make that case last.

These kinds of cultural reference points mean something to us. We seek them out over and over again—whether that is watching episodes of television shows, purchasing the same product over and over again, or reading someone's daily blog posts. They give us something to look forward to and our engagement with this content helps contribute to the creation of our identities.

And *Dooce*—and other blogs like it—are no different.

Over the course of nearly 20 years and more than 8,000 blog posts, Armstrong has shared stories about her life, her kids, her personal struggles with depression, and her separation.

This has allowed her to tap into something universal to her followers—the personal experiences of life. You know, those things we can all relate to. And her approach to discussing these things helps make some of the more difficult topics manageable. Her ability to find humor in tough situations makes them relatable and feel less "heavy."

It has also created a sense of intimacy between Armstrong and her followers. Despite the fact that many of them have never met Armstrong, her personal way of communicating imbues her content with the sense that she is sharing a personal story with just you, the reader.

Armstrong's story exemplifies how influencers build relationships with their readership—and that these relationships can be incredibly close despite influencers and their followers never having met one another.

But what makes an influencer influential to their followers? Armstrong's story elucidates pieces of why this is, but let's take a step back to understand this relationship a bit more. This will be the focus of the rest of this chapter.

What Makes an Influencer Influential?

You may have seen a lot written about influencers that would have you believe that someone needs a large following to be considered one.[40]

Certainly, many of the most popular influencers out there, indeed, have large followings, but are they influential because they have large followings, or do they have large followings because they are influential. And if it is the latter, what makes them influential to begin with?

Well, in fact, I believe that there has been an overemphasis on the importance of follower size in the industry historically. Many social media users have been focused on growing one's following as a primary goal, and most social media platforms emphasize follower size as a key metric.

Moreover, paid influencer marketing has only served to exacerbate this perception that follower size is important. As more brands enter the marketplace paying influencers to promote products and services, influencers are able to command more money if they have more followers. This, in turn, has resulted in such nefarious practices as influencers buying followers to boost their perceived reach in order to be paid more when working with brands.[41] And this is rampant in the industry today. According to a report by AdAge, brands such as Pampers and Olay ranked 4th and 10th, respectively, on a list of brands which have the most fake followers among their paid influencers. Ritz-Carlton topped the list with a whopping 78 percent of its influencers' followers being reported as fake.[42]

Thus, it *would* seem that the size of one's following really is important to determining how influential one is.

But follower size is not the only metric by which you can, and should, assess an influencer's level of influence. In fact, it is arguably not even a worthwhile metric to use to assess this. As Gini Dietrich says in her article entitled, "The Good, the Bad, and the Ugly of Influencer Marketing,"

> You see an influencer isn't an influencer because of mere numbers. It's about their connection with their audience and how they communicate with them. Bigger isn't always better.[43]

So if follower size does not make an influencer influential, then what does?

Well, we learned in Chapter 1 that opinion leaders are influential because often they are similar to those whom they are trying to influence. We saw this in the case of Heather Armstrong where she wrote about things that both she and her readers had experienced and that helped them to relate to her.

Armstrong's relatability was not just something that was good for growing her following, or driving hundreds of comments on posts; it also resulted in Armstrong establishing credibility with her readers. The trust that Armstrong has established with her readers thus allows her to become an authority on topics that she was perceived to be knowledgeable about.

It is well established that influencers who focus on one particular subject, such as parenting, food, or travel, will often be perceived to have more authority on that particular topic. This, in turn, means that when they are endorsing a brand or product, their perceived expertise lends authority to that brand or product.

Findings from my own research back this up. The influencers I met over the course of my research shared that indeed their followers are similar to them. Yasmin was a 46-year-old Hispanic running and mommy influencer I met who agreed that "[her] readers are like [her]."

All the influencers I interviewed and surveyed thought that this had to do with what they have in common: they are all moms or parents, they all have similar interests like fitness or running, and/or they are all located in the same area geographically. As Emma, a 35-year-old Hispanic entertainment and technology influencer I met during my research, said,

> I refer to them as friends. Most are moms and dads, so they are going through similar experiences.

As a result, this similarity meant that their followers often sought advice from them and wanted their opinions about things, ultimately embuing them with credibility. As Theresa, another influencer I met during the course of my research, shared,

> They ask me a ton of questions and seek my opinion. You get more practical advice from people who are your peers in that situation.

However, theory (and Chapter 1) tell us that it is not just similarity between an influencer and his/her followers that contributes to how influential he or she is. In addition to similarity, it has also been theorized that the influence between individuals is stronger when they interact frequently.[44]

For instance, online influencers are followed by an audience with whom they have established a relationship over time. This relationship has evolved out of multiple and frequent interactions between influencers and their audience members, which can take the forms of likes, shares, and retweets of a post, comments on a post, and private messages via social media and email, over that time period. And often these interactions take place on a weekly, daily, or even, hourly basis.

In my research, I explored how frequently influencers interacted with their followers, finding that most of them interact daily or every other day with them. For instance, Molly, a 38-year-old Caucasian sexual health influencer I met, said,

> I usually communicate with at least one [follower] every day, sometimes twenty or thirty.

Yasmin shared that she sees her followers at her races, and Leigh, a 34-year-old Caucasian lifestyle and parenting influencer I met, also said,

> I do have a few [readers] that I know and interact with … I text with them.

Related to this, I also explored how these frequent interactions contribute to perceptions of clsoeness, finding that these multiple and frequent interactions contribute to a stronger sense of connection between the follower, the topic, the influencer, and the other followers; and this, thereby, helps reinforce their identities. For example, Jacinda, a 40-year-old Hispanic health and finance influencer I met, said,

> I talk to them a lot. I am really engaged with them. They are really honest relationships.

As well, Monique, a 39-year-old African American/Black fitness and health influencer I met, shared.

> Readers ask questions and send messages via social media, [blog] comments, and email daily or every other day. I feel close with my readers. I have never met them in person, but they will remember other stories [I have written about] and will comment on them and make a connection to them. They hold me accountable.

Ultimately, there are all sorts of influencers, and they range in topic and popularity and the platforms on which they communicate. Consistent across these though are the characteristics that make them influential in the first place—and overwhelmingly, those characteristics have to do with similarity and frequency of contact. These characteristics serve to strengthen the bonds between influencers and their followers. In the literature, connections that are characterized this way are often referred to as "strong ties," which is a concept that we will discuss more a bit later in this chapter as well as in subsequent chapters.

As we will see, though, this world of online influencers has been undergoing some substantial shifts—and continues to do so. And these changes are affecting the relationships with their followers. Strong ties still exist, but not all relationships can be characterized in this manner.

Understanding these shifts is critical to understanding how this industry operates today and how you can work with these influencers to promote your message, product, or service. This is the focus of the next section.

Nothing Endures but Change

Almost universally, the influencers I met through my research said that they started their blogs as personal online journals and as a means to stay in touch with friends and family.

The mothers in the group stated that in the beginning, they often used their blogs to document their lives with their children—especially if they lived far away from the rest of their family. As Eve, a 29-year-old, Asian, healthy living, and lifestyle influencer I met, said,

> I moved across the country. I used to live in California and came to the East Coast for my Master's degree. I started a blog to keep in touch with friends. I always liked writing and keeping a journal.

Because of this, many of them stated that, early on, they did not actively promote their content beyond their personal social networks. They were for a small and finite group of people whom they knew personally. And there was really no interest in expanding that followership.

However, as we have already noted, this world of online influencers is changing. In this new environment, as we have been discussing, influencers are regularly paid to endorse products and share messages. Moreover, much of this change has happened just recently, in about the last 5 years. Over the course of this time, influencers have seen what was once an informal community of writers shift into a more business-oriented and brand-driven one. As Emma noted,

> Blogging now is not like blogging five years ago, everyone now has a business card, everyone has a media kit.

Driving this change has been the rise of media companies that are solely focused on managing networks of hundreds of thousands of influencers. The sole purpose of these companies is to bring together brands and influencers around common interests—for instance, a travel influencer can help promote a new vacation destination, a food blogger can help support the release of a new food product or the launch of a new restaurant, and a fashion influencer can help drive online sales of the new fall line.

All participants I talked with during the course of my research reported belonging to at least one such network, with most reporting belonging to multiple. Common networks that they reported belonging to were BlogHer, Mom 2.0, and Blogalicious.

This fact—that media companies have arisen to help monetize the content of hundreds of thousands of influencers—means that the once independent and informal relationships that existed are now being replaced by a new type of relationship—one that is symbiotic. In this new type of relationship, brands get their messages disseminated via trusted voices and influencers make money off of their reputation with their followers.

And I cannot emphasize enough how important these changes are. Influencer marketing is now a multibillion-dollar industry. In the United States alone, as of 2018, the industry has made nearly $27 billion in ad sales.[45]

As a result of this shift in the types of relationships that exist, content that was at one time comprised entirely of honest and personal experiences is now increasingly comprised of posts that have been curated and paid for by brands and campaigns. Moreover, this plethora of paid ads also means that campaigns and brands are determining much of the content audiences see and engage with online every day.

And many of the influencers I talked with during the course of my research conveyed this same sentiment. They acknowledged that they do not post like they used to. They do not talk about their children as much as they used to. And almost all of them shared that branded paid campaigns are now a regular part of their content.

As a result, this has changed how they view their content. They see their posts more as business-oriented, and much less personal. As Melanie shared,

> As my readership grew, the writing became less personal. Some blogs are really personalized, but I lessen this.

Maria, a 44-year-old Hispanic mommy and travel influencer I met, also shared,

> In the old blog, it was really personal. With this new direction, it's more business and not as personal. It uses personal anecdotes, but I keep it more objective … [I won't write about things like] personal women's health or perimenopause. I don't know if I can go there myself. It's too personal.

Finally, even Heather Armstrong has noted this trend, saying,

> Especially as they've gotten older, I've been much more careful. The story of a child from zero to three

> is pretty universal—kicking, screaming, pooping, not pooping. As they develop their own little quirks and personalities, I've worked hard to protect them. People think I reveal 95 percent of my life when it's really only around 5 percent. My older daughter is eleven, and now I won't write anything about her on Dooce without her reading it first. They're both completely aware of what I do. Their friends read Dooce, their teachers read Dooce, our neighbors read Dooce.

So what does this shift mean? Well, this rise in the number of sponsored posts has had several repercussions.

First and foremost, while the *quantity* of content that is online nowadays is increasing, the amount of original content that is being created in decreasing. As a result, the *quality* of content has gone down. As Melanie, a 39-year-old Hispanic mommy, lifestyle, and travel influencer I met, said,

> Most blogs are just jumping from sponsorship to sponsorship which dilutes the quality of the blog.

Additionally, a substantial side effect of this trend is that it has resulted in influencers feeling like they have to present a certain standard or convey a certain look to their followers. The influencers I met in my research often commented that they feel like they have to be "on all the time" and "killing it" with fresh, "Pinterest-pretty" content. Yasmin said,

> Online personas have to be on and killing it all the time. They never show flaws.

Armstrong also noted this, stating,

> Now, a lot of mommy blogs are about documenting instead of storytelling. It's a photo essay of their kid sitting on the countertop in perfectly clean clothes licking the cake spoon. It's so curated. In the beginning, it was all mess. People were craving honest stories about parenting. I think people are craving that

> again now, but bloggers are afraid to be that honest. Since blogging is so flush with money, the immediate thought is, is there going to be money in that? How do you monetize a mess?

This has made some influencers feel as if unattainable goals are being set, with some influencers presenting one persona online and another offline. This creates a world where, as Sam, a 49-year-old Caucasian influencer I met, said,

> "It's hard to know what's real" and what is not

Sam told me a couple of stories that get at this very point. The first story was about how she learned that none of the pictures on a Do-It-Yourself (DIY) blog were actually photos from projects the influencer had done herself. While the influencer did disclose this, it was done in such a way that the average follower could easily miss the disclosure thereby allowing the follower to create his or her own assumptions about the projects the influencer was showcasing.

The other story Sam told me was about a fashion influencer she knew who would go out and buy clothes that she would try on and take pictures of in order to promote them on her blog. After she posted her content, though, she would return the items. So consumers were seeing the posts and clicking on the website links to purchase the items despite the fact that the influencer was not, in fact, actually using the products she was endorsing. Sam said,

> Generally, I don't think that the public understands these kinds of tactics. Bloggers who go buy clothes, take pictures, and then go return them. All to drive sales artificially.

These occurrences are also changing how followers interact with influencers. For instance, influencers, who may have once known some or all of their followers personally, can no longer do so. As well, influencers are not getting as many blog comments or as many direct questions from their followers as they once did.

So that frequency of contact that is so important to the strength of the influencer-follower relationship (that we referenced earlier) is hard to maintain in this new environment.

Indeed, much of that one-to-one relationship has been lost.

And while influencers and their followers still coalesce around a topic or set of topics that they both are interested in, by these standards, it would appear that perceptions by followers of influencers' credibility and expertise would be declining, thereby weakening the relationship.

I know, I have painted a dim picture here. But all is not lost because there are also influencers who are rebelling against these shifts and this is helping to maintain the credibility of the industry. This is what the next section is about.

Influencing Disruption

So yeah, after that last section, you might be thinking to yourself that this industry is just a depressing mess that is not worth investing in.

But, as I mentioned, it is not all bad. The story does not end here.

Rather, many influencers are, in fact, striving to bring authenticity back to blogging and social media and thereby, reinvigorate the relationships they have with their followers.

So we find ourselves—or I should say, influencers find themselves—at a crossroads today. The industry is heavily networked and monetized and that drives much of the content that is shared online. But not everyone has drunk the Kool-Aid. This new business-oriented world seems to have pushed influencers into one of two categories—either adapting to these business practices or rebelling against them.

For those who are resisting these practices, they tend to refer to themselves as "rebel bloggers." These truly see themselves as opinion leaders for their followers, and because of this, they feel that they have a certain responsibility to them.

They want to continue to deliver high-quality, original content to their followers—not just paid content that they are contracted to write.

They also want to show "all the dirty parts." They do not want to present an image that is unattainable. As Amanda, a 34-year-old Caucasian parenting and lifestyle influencer I met, said,

> I have been blogging for over seven years. It reflects all the changes over those seven years. I like to talk about my blog as 'not Pinterest-pretty'. I show all the messes … Life changes, kids … how life evolves and you have to roll with it.

They are showing their imperfections, and they are creating a more humble and true sense of the lives of influencers. As Sara, a Hispanic mommy, lifestyle, and travel influencer I met, said,

> I try my best to build a relationship with my readers by sharing my own personal experiences and/or struggles with them. I feel that sometimes that is the best way for them to feel like they 'know' me.

Because they are doing this, their followers are identifying with the issues that they read about and they are trusting that these influencers are giving them an authentic portrayal of the topic at hand. And it is working! Because, despite the overall decline in blog comments, those who are really invested with their followers say that they still get a lot of questions from them. As Theresa said,

> If bloggers share personal details about themselves regularly and often, then readers will do so too.

Ultimately, they are attempting to disrupt an industry that is focused on curating a pretty narrative, but one that is not always real.

Thus, it is within this subgroup of influencers where strong relationships, or strong ties as we have been calling them, still exist. They are still creating deep connections with their followers. They are able to connect with them on a real and human level and this establishes trust and imbues their content with credibility.

And by working with these individuals who have become experts in an area, marketers can still tap into this credibility on a topic to promote products and services to consumers, arguably more successfully than working with influencers who have large followings but who also only post paid content. Maybe they are parents who have gone through the birth of their first child and know the struggles of new parenthood; or maybe they have many children and can speak knowledgeably to the challenges of parenting multiples. Maybe they have just been diagnosed with cancer or they are a survivor, and can talk about their experiences with treatments, hospitals and side effects. Maybe they have just lost a lot of weight or are in the process of doing so, and they can talk about the challenges they faced and the strategies they used to keep them on track.

Regardless of the person or topic you are talking about, influencers have a lived experience, which gives their words and recommendations credence—if they choose to share that experience. And followers trust that. It is like they're saying, "I've been there—and this is how I got through it." Only they are saying it about millions of topics to millions of people.

And that is why marketers and advertisers who work with these kinds of influencers see such high returns. In fact, as of 2016, marketers from across a wide variety of industries reported that, on average, they received 11.69 U.S. dollars of value for every dollar they spent on paid influencer marketing.[46]

Final Reflections

This chapter reveals insights into the world of online influencers, why they are influential, and how this world is quickly evolving. Money is shifting the influencer ethos—and because of this, we are seeing a tension between transparency and the evolution of a new marketplace, which is having substantial effects on the relationships influencers have with their followers.

But influencer-to-influencer relationships are also changing and in order to understand the nature of these relationships, it is worth some discussion of the larger business context of this influencer ethos, e.g., how it operates and who the players are. This is the focus of the next chapter.

Chapter 3

The Business of Relationships

re·la·tion·ship | /rəˈlāSH(ə)nˌSHip/ | noun

The way in which two or more concepts, objects, or people are connected, or the state of being connected.

As I have mentioned, the world of influencer marketing is made up of hundreds of thousands of individual influencers. And many of them belong to networks that help connect brands with these influencers and their followers. These networks are shaping this industry into what it is today—and will become in the future.

But this was not always the case. The early days of blogging were unstructured and technologically limited. Blogs were new-ish. Social media, as we know it today, did not exist. Paid social ads did not exist. Unique URLs were not heavily used yet.

But for the pioneers of the day, those things did not matter. They were doing this out of curiosity, for community, and because they were passionate about whatever it was they were blogging about.

Their work, their mistakes, and their successes would help build the foundation for the world we know today.

One of these pioneers was Cooper Munroe. She eventually went on to found and run The Motherhood, one of the oldest and largest mom and parenting networks around. But at the time, she was just someone who was starting a blog.

Cooper started her blog in the early 2000s.[47] Prior to this, weblogs had started popping up and journals like Newsweek were featuring sections in their publications called, "Excerpts from the Blog." However, most of these pieces featured white men writing about technology and politics. There was no diversity. There were few, if any, women writing blogs at this time. There were hardly any female voices at all. And, certainly, there were no moms writing blogs. It was a singular perspective about only a few topics.

Yes, certain women's communities were flourishing at this time but women's magazines, and other similar forms of communication, did not seem to align with the everyday woman's experience. For example, if you bought a women's magazine-of-the-day, it was highly likely that you'd see an article entitled, a "24-Step Process to Breast Feeding," but the piece would have been written by someone just out of college.

So it was a new world for women's voices, and the few who had decided to start a blog were brave. For those women who were blogging, they were sharing stories about their lives in ways that had never really been done before.

At the same time as these blogs were popping up, communities and everyday-life connections were also changing. People were becoming more mobile. As a result, people were not living next door to family or maintaining strong connections to the communities where they lived as they once had. Relationships were distant. Where once generations of women (mothers, daughters, aunts, and grandmothers) would often sit around the kitchen table drinking coffee and talking; now, if you needed support or community, you had to go out and find it.

Considering these things collectively, this time period was unique. There were few female voices online, and the ones that did exist tended to be more corporate-type websites.

And these did not really represent the everyday woman's experience. As well, people, specifically women, were seeking out connections with others that were less and less available in their physical neighborhoods and communities.

And while today, many argue that the Internet may be negatively impacting relationships, it was, in fact the Internet that provided the solution to the challenges of those early days.

It was because of the advent of the Internet and the emergence of weblogs that more and more women began building online communities to address this need. And in these communities, women began sharing their stories and building strong relationships. They began to showcase how they were the experts in their own lives.

And of all the women who were actively self-organizing online at this time, the first group to really do this was the moms. It was revolutionary to say the least.

Yet, despite their cutting-edge vision for cultivating a community of moms online, these pioneering bloggers were often not fully appreciated. In fact, many of the early articles about the emerging world of the "mommy blogger" were often considered disparaging.

Then, in 2005, immediately after Hurricane Katrina hit the Gulf Coast, federal relief efforts were failing. So this small but mighty world of women bloggers began organizing to help.

And Cooper was one of them.

In response to what was going on, she decided to write a blog post about getting donations to the Gulf Coast. But remember, this was not the technologically connected world influencers operate in today. There was no Facebook or Twitter. Cooper did not even have a unique URL for the blog.

Because of this, she thought they'd maybe get a couple of responses to this post, but instead—and to Cooper's great surprise—they got tens of thousands of them. They received so many that the blog crashed.

This moment crystallized for Cooper how powerful these communities and networks really were—and were going to be in the future. When there was a problem, there were people who were so connected that they could be quickly organized to help solve the problem. And technology enabled that connection. In this case, this had been a completely female-driven initiative, and it had been immensely successful.

Moreover, at a time when the meaning of "community" was changing, it was a strong reminder of what true community really meant—it didn't require any longer that people be face-to-face to have a strong sense of community; rather, it meant people finding each other and coming together around a common cause, issue, or passion.

In fact, it did appear that this network of bloggers was really like a community. A neighborhood. So Cooper created The Motherhood modeling it on this idea. Her aim? To build an online community for women and moms from all walks of life to come together around the issues they care about most.

Today, that same mission guides the network. It touts more than 3,000 members and more than 500 campaigns nationwide. However, it now operates in a very different environment, one that is more organized, monetized, and commoditized. And this new environment is shifting the relationships influencers have with *other influencers.*

Thus far, we have focused on influencer relationships with followers, but, the business of working with influencers, the relationships between these influencers, and how these are changing is also important to understand as you venture into this space. These things are the focus of the rest of this chapter.

Influencers as Brands

To understand the business of influencers first requires a discussion of how influencers see themselves as brands.

Every influencer I have ever met or worked with thinks of themselves not just as a blogger or a social media influencer, but, rather, as a brand. They have an area of focus for their content—be that parenting, health, running, DIY or some other topic—and their online presence is imbued with that focus. It shows up on their blog, their social media, their podcast (if they have one), and their e-newsletters. They also have a particular look and feel to their online presence. Maybe it is bright and cheery. Maybe it is "green." Maybe it is crisp and clean.

Whatever the area of focus and look and feel are, these attributes are not just randomly selected. Rather, they are curated by the influencers. They express who they are, what they are passionate about, and permeate all their public communications.

The focus on one's brand also often leads to the curation of a particular type of audience that often aligns with that brand. For instance, Elle, a 42-year-old Hispanic crafting influencer, I met during my research shared that her focus on crafting has led her to have a number of Evangelical Christians among her followership.

This, therefore, means that when influencers are selecting topics to write about, this brand and their audience are always front and center in deciding what to share—and what not to. As Carol, a 44-year-old African American wine, Black hair, and lifestyle influencer who I met, shared,

> It needs to have relevance to your brand.

For Elle, the fact that her brand has attracted a particular audience makes it hard for her to talk about certain topics openly on her blog. For instance, her personal interest is in sexual health, but she knows that her followers do not really want to see this kind of content from her.

These factors have led her to differentiate between how she is in her personal life and what she shares on her blog. Because of this, anything health-related needs to tie directly into the brand she has on her blog. If it does not, it appears off-brand and inauthentic. Moreover, the topic could also offend a large swath of her followership.

The significance of a topic to an influencer's brand and how that topic reinforces—or does not—that influencer's brand are central to their decision-making process about whether or not to communicate a particular message. This means that if you are asking an influencer to write about something that is not what they normally talk about, finding a way to connect the two topics is critical. An influencer will not typically write about something that feels off-brand.

The idea that influencers see themselves as brands is also connected to two other related topics—networking and payment. We will discuss these next.

Networking: Why Is It Important?

Every year, hundreds of social media, and specifically online influencer, conferences are held all around the globe.[48] Some of these are influencer-only, while others are for both brands and influencers. And even at the some of the larger brand-influencer conferences, there will be dedicated time for influencer-only discussions.

Interacting with fellow participants at these events is not only about exchanging information, but also about building your professional network. If you are an influencer, you can raise the visibility of your blog or social media at these events through presentations and participating in the discussions and events that take place.

As well, for influencers—both new and old—conferences are a great (and often the only) opportunity to meet CEOs, CMOs, and high-level managers representing the world's leading companies, brands, and campaigns. They are valuable places to introduce yourself to the people who are designing campaigns and show how you can be a part of them.

As a brand or campaign—especially if you are new to the influencer world—you can meet influencers who you might want to work with and learn about the latest and greatest trends happening in the industry. You can also reconnect with influencers who you have met before and continue to build those relationships. Finally, you can also keep tabs on what your competition is doing in order to adjust and amplify your own strategy.

Most of these networks make event presentations, photos, and quotes from participants available online, which is an additional marketing opportunity for you—whether you are a brand or an influencer. If you presented, you can syndicate your online content via your website, blog, and social media. If you were in attendance, you can help promote others' content and thereby, make virtual connections with them that can last well past the duration of the actual event.

Related to this, there are additional opportunities to continue to the conversations virtually following these events. Influencers tend to get together in virtual groups on platforms such as Facebook. For brands and campaigns, Facebook offers Groups for Pages, which lets brands create Groups that are linked to their business page. These Groups give brands a space to engage with their community organically and in a more in-depth manner. For example, Instant Pot uses their Group as a recipe-sharing space.[49]

Indeed, many of the networks I have mentioned previously, e.g., Mom 2.0 and BlogHer, already have established groups for information sharing and networking. Often, virtual groups are created specifically for each iteration of a conference or event, e.g., Mom 2.0 has separate groups for each year of their annual conference.

So there are numerous opportunities and ways to connect with brands and influencers—and most of these focus on perpetuating the business of working with influencers. While it would be nice to believe that people participate in this industry and these events just to learn and grow, that is not always the case. It may be part of it but really, making money is a primary driver of this activity. It is a business after all.

While money may be an uncomfortable topic for some, it is an important one to talk about as it relates to working with influencers. This is, after all, a multibillion-dollar business. This is the topic of the next section.

The Uncomfortable Topic of "Payment"

We've talked at length about how influencers are operating more as businesses now than they did before. I have also mentioned how many of these influencers now have media kits and belong to a number of professional networks that help them get connected to brands, campaigns, and other influencers. Well, a main reason for this is to make money.

The topic of payment is a really important aspect of this industry, so it is important to understand the mechanisms through which influencers can earn money. There are many possible ways for influencers to do this off of their blogs and social media. For instance, one method is using Google AdSense. Google AdSense allows for clickable text-based, image, video, or interactive media advertisements to show up across blogs and websites. These are targeted by site content and audience, and when these ads are seen and/or clicked by followers, the blog or website owner earns money.[49]

But as it relates to direct payment to influencers to promote a message or product, there are essentially two main ways that an influencer can get paid.

The first is that they can receive a lump sum for writing a blog post or sharing a message in social media. Rates differ based on the reach and notoriety of the influencer and what is being asked of them. Generally speaking, writing a blog post will be more expensive because it is longer-form content and takes more time to do. A post in social media, otherwise known as a "social share," is a bit more turnkey for influencers—especially if you give them content that they can easily post with little to no editing. Because of this, these often cost less.

The second way influencers can get paid—and one, which has seen substantial growth over the years—is something called affiliate marketing. Affiliate marketing refers to,

> A merchant [that creates] a network of affiliate organizations [e.g., influencers] that refer customers to its site. Many merchants pay affiliates a referral fee for every referral that is converted into a customer.[50]

One of the largest affiliate programs is with Amazon, but most large retailers and brands have affiliate marketing programs. Through their blog and social media posts, influencer affiliates help drive customers to a website for purchase, for which, influencers are paid an agreed upon commission amount.[51] Amazon boasts more than 900,000 affiliates and pays its affiliates up to 15 percent commission on sales.

As mentioned, payment is now a regular part of the influencer marketing industry. So the bottom line is this: Expect to pay or get requests for payment. This is the business model now.

It is worth mentioning here that, while payment is now the norm, *if* the topic is interesting enough, you may be able to engage influencers to share your messages without paying them. But you should be honest and upfront about what your budget allows. Influencers are willing to work with you on what you can offer—especially if it is a topic that is important to them.

If you cannot pay—or cannot pay much—consider what else you can offer to "sweeten the deal." Consider exclusive opportunities that only influencers will get to do, or new creative or campaign messaging that they can help launch. Anything that is uniquely for them, is not widely available, and gives them an exclusive behind-the-scene look at something that they can help unveil and share with the rest of the world is also considered currency for influencers.

Finally, in the spirit of building long relationships, consider what the future may hold for them. Perhaps you cannot pay now, but maybe in the future you will be able to.

Despite the commonplace practice of paying influencers and the widespread use of afflliliate links, consumers are not always aware of these practices. And this raises an important issue related to payment—that of the disclosure. We will tackle this next.

Payment Disclosures

The concept of disclosures, as it relates to influencers, refers to truthfully revealing any relationships between influencers and the brands they work with. Historically, these relationships have been hard to tease out. They have either been vaguely disclsosed or not disclosed at all. Given this, the Federal Trade Commission (FTC) released guidelines that provide loose direction about when disclosure language is required.

The FTC's disclosure guidelines refer to language that influencers must include in their posts to clarifies the nature of their work with an advertiser. These regulations apply to anyone who produces online content about brands in exchange for compensation. Compensation includes cash, but it also can include receipt of free products/services, discounts, special access to something, and/or the exchange of other goods or services. If an influencer has purchased the product on his or her own, there is no need to disclose anything. As well, anything done pro bono does not fall under these regulations, although there may still be ethical reasons to disclose non-paid relationships. The FTC only regulates endorsements that are made on behalf of a paying advertiser.[52]

Disclosures can take the form of a lengthy statement on a blog post or a short hashtag, e.g., #ad, #client, and #sponsored, in a social media post. As well, while Facebook, Instagram, and other social media platforms provide branded content tools that provide additional identification of sponsored posts; it is worth noting that the FTC does not consider these tools adequate for disclosure.[53] These guidelines can be a little murky so to help you; below is a cheat sheet that may help you understand how you should think about disclosures for your own work.

FTC Disclosure Guidelines Cheat Sheet[a]

[a] www.ftc.gov/news-events/blogs/business-blog/2017/09/three-ftc-actions-interest-influencers.

Generally speaking, reputable influencers will disclose on their blog or social media that they will receive a commission from purchases made via the links they are sharing (or that they will receive a payment for a particular post), but this is not universally done.

According to a 2018 report by eMarketer, "more than four in 10 influencers said they label their content as #sponsored or #ad only when they are asked to." Some people worry that including disclosure language will lead to decreased engagement, but data suggest that consumers, in fact, appreciate this transparency and honesty from marketers and influencers. Moreover, not disclosing payments can put influencers and their marketing teams at risk for FTC scrutiny and consumer backlash. So the bottom line is this—disclosing paid relationships is worth it. So just do it.

Payment—including the disclosures of payment—is now an important part of working with influencers. Moreover, payment has affected relationships between influencers. Understanding this is important to be able to set and manage expectations with influencers, brands, and campaigns. This is the focus of the next section.

The Changing Nature of The Relationships Influencers Have With Each Other

The early days of blogging saw a lot of collaboration between influencers. We saw this in the earlier story about Cooper Munroe and how she mobilized women to help with donations to the victims of Hurricane Katrina.

And there are many other stories like this from across the influencer world.

One example comes from the blog, Mommy Mafia Miami, which was started, and still is written by, a group of women friends in Miami. Their story goes something like this.

As young women, these three friends would often gather for 4:00 a.m. nightcaps after a night out on the town. These gatherings were a place for chatting, laughing, and recapping the evening.

But as their lives changed and they got married and had children, those 4 a.m. nightcaps turned into 4 a.m. feedings.[54] And with these life changes also came changes to the content of their conversations. Now, their typical conversations covered topics such as pregnancy, co-sleeping, school selection, and books.

Yet, while the content of those conversations changed, the act of sharing and supporting one another did not. These women still shared their joys and their struggles with each other and in doing so, realized something important—

> [How amazing it is that] one can get more information in an hour with three other Mafia Mommies than… in three hours behind a computer searching on Google.

So it was with this change in relationship and these new types of conversations that a new business idea—and Mommy Mafia Miami—was born.

Just as The Motherhood was created with the aim of connecting women and moms, this co-written blog was also created as a place to connect moms specifically in Miami and achieve this same kind of sharing. A space for moms by moms, it allowed women to vent about the stresses of "mommyhood" and "wifehood" but also share their expertise and knowledge about the best kid-related topics tailored to a Miami audience.

The origin stories of The Motherhood and Mommy Mafia Miami exemplify how influencers often know each other and share and learn from each other in real life. Moreover, especially in the early days of blogging, these close connections often lead to other types of partnerships that happen online.

However, as we have been discussing, the shifts that are occurring in the world of influencer marketing are causing a whole host of other changes. And among these are the changing relationships between influencers, themselves.

A primary change that the industry is seeing that I came across in my research is that many influencers now consume substantially less content written by other influencers than they used to. As Melanie, a 39-year-old Hispanic mommy, lifestyle, and travel influencer I met, said,

> Maybe in the beginning…I read a lot more blogs than I do now.

Whereas Mommy Mafia Miami evolved as a joint effort between influencers, there are now fewer and fewer of these types of efforts. This appears to be a result of the fact that influencers seem to feel that there is less to learn from each other. And this sentiment can be directly tied to the fact that so many influencer feeds are now filled primarily with paid promotions.

This fact is exacerbated by the fact that, often, influencers who have similar interests participate in the same campaigns. For example, if a brand runs a campaign targeted to new moms, it is highly likely that all the influencers they recruit to participate in that campaign will be moms themselves. This results in a group of mom bloggers sharing the same content. If this is happening often—and it is because we know that the number of paid posts is increasing—it results in little new information being shared by one influencer that another influencer can learn from.

Thus, as we have seen, the emergence of paid posts is restructuring influencer approaches to content, and this restructuring of content is resulting in the creation of a body of work that is increasingly less interesting to other influencers. This, therefore, is changing the relationships between influencers.

Similar to the trend with influencer-follower relationships, however, the rebellious part of the industry is trying to get back to those close relationships from the early days. For instance, Sara, a Hispanic mommy, lifestyle, and travel influencer I met during the course of my research, said that she is well networked with other influencers and enjoys finding likeminded influencers through these networks, especially Christian mothers. As well, Maria, a 44-year-old Hispanic mommy and travel influencer, said that she meets with her influencer friends' in-person daily.

While this might generally appear to be a good thing, a potential side effect of this, however, is that it may create really strong subgroups comprised entirely of like-minded influencers (as seen in Sara's connection to other Christian mothers).

You will recall that we briefly discussed the concept of "strong ties" in Chapter 2. The value of strong ties, as we mentioned, is that they can be incredibly influential to one another because they are similar and spend time together. However, a drawback of this is that little new information gets shared between these kinds of relationships.

To ensure that new information can be shared with individuals, "weak ties" are needed. "Weak ties" are the counterpoint to the concept of "strong ties." "Weak ties" refer to those connections with individuals who are less similar to us and with whom we are less close. Because of these differences, however, it is most often through these relationships where innovation and new ideas can be shared.

Therefore, while this group of influencers may be trying to rebuild the kinds of relationships that influencers used to have with one another, by connecting and learning only from influencers who are similar to them, in fact, not much learning can take place. This may lead to misinformation or skewed perspectives on topics and it may mean that information these groups have does not make it to others who are not part of these groups.

Overall, while we want more of these strong tie relationships to return, connecting *only* with strong ties is still limiting. It limits the reach of influencers. It also limits their influence. Finally, it limits their roles as opinion leaders. It is easy to sway likeminded people's opinions; it is another thing all together to sway the opinions of those who are different from us. Thus collaborations with "weak ties" are still important and can help counter these issues.

These networks and communities are all about relationships, and these relationships are changing. Influencers' willingness to consume less content from other influencers signals less collaboration and sharing. For those who are trying to collaborate more, they are often seeking out only likeminded individuals. This may stunt new information from being shared and limit their roles as opinion leaders. There may also be opportunities to change this, however, if new ideas and new information can be introduced into these likeminded circles. We will tackle this more in the next chapter.

However, before we turn our attention to the topic of Chapter 4, let's review a few best practices that can help you understand the business of influencers and how to take advantage of this industry to achieve your communication and marketing goals. Below are some tips for working with influencers and influencer networks.

Tips for Communicators

At this point, you may be all excited to start researching influencers in the hope that you can engage some of them to support your initiative. However, before you begin doing so, you need to do a few things first.

Identify Your Goals

A first step that you should take before beginning to reach out to influencers is identifying your goals.

To do this, you want to be really clear about what you want to achieve and set specific and measurable goals. For example, rather than just setting a goal to "increase brand awareness," you might set a goal to "get at least 15k impressions" on an influencer's post. You can also set other types of measureable goals, such as the following:

- Achieve a certain number of social media engagement (e.g., likes, shares, or comments)
- Drive a certain percentage increase in traffic to your website traffic (e.g., how many visitors did an influencer's post drive to your site?)
- Achieve a certain number or percentage of conversions (e.g., how many sales or sign-ups resulted from the campaign?)
- Achieve a certain amount of revenue from the campaign (which would require some sort of e-commerce functionality and/or a traceable connection between an online promotion and an offline purchase)

Identifying Influencers

Once you have set your goals, you need to find some influencers that can and are willing to support your initiative. There are three basic routes you can take to find influencers. First, you can manually search via Google, Facebook, and other social media sites. You can also work with a network, like one of the ones mentioned in this book.

An alternative approach is to use influencer identification tools.[55] These are databases of bloggers and social media influencers that can be easily searched in order to create a list of possible influencers for your campaign.

Moreover, there are dozens of these kinds of databases available to you, but they range in terms of cost from free to multiple thousands of dollars a month. See Table 3.1 for a comparison of some of these tools.

Table 3.1 Influencer ID Tools[a]

Tool	*Free Version?*	*Price Range*	*Blogs*	*Twitter*	*Instagram*	*Facebook*	*YouTube*
Followerwonk	X	$		X			
Trendspottr		$			X		
AuthoritySpy		$	X				
Buzzsumo	X	$$	X	X	X	X	X
Klear	X	$$	X	X	X	X	X
Fresh Press Media		$$	X	X	X	X	X
Upfluence		$$$	X	X	X	X	X
GroupHigh		$$$	X	X	X	X	X
TapInfluence		$$$	X	X	X	X	X
HYPR		$$$	X	X	X	X	X

[a] www.theleverageway.com/blog/influencer-identification-tools-find-brand-partners/.

Vetting Your List of Influencers

Once you have identified a list of possible influencers, it is important to closely vet them.

To do this well, you want to make sure you've identified a set of detailed criteria by which you will assess your list. Such criteria could include audience demographics, follower size, how political they are, the age of their children or the children of their followers, or whether they are open to doing unpaid posts. Then, once you have established the criteria against which you will vet the list, you want to evaluate them on each of those points.

This means that you need to not just read their bio and some of their posts, but you should get to know them really well, follow their content, subscribe to their e-newsletters, and do a deep dive into their content. You want to review all the content on influencers' profiles, including archived content. This part of the vetting process is really important and aims to identify any hidden "red flags" that may exist in historical content posted by the influencer.

To do this appropriately, you need to be aware of what a "red flag" is for you or for your client. This could be political orientation or being anti-vaccine. It could be a bad purchase experience at a particular retailer or an angry customer service rant. Red flags will shift depending on what sensitivities you or your clients have, but it is important to understand these up front, identify them ahead of time, and look for them across all influencer content before beginning to talk with any influencers.

I cannot emphasize this enough—you do not want to skimp on this step because if you miss something, it could result in a really bad interaction with an influencer. In fact, to emphasize just how important this part of the process is, let me share a quick story with you from my own experience about how bad it can really be if you <u>do not</u> do your homework.

Back in the early days of influencer marketing—when it was not called influencer marketing (we called it "organic marketing" back then)—I was working for the largest independent media company in the United States, called Horizon Media. I was part of a team focused solely on social media that was comprised of me, my boss who led the group, and a number of junior staff who helped manage and support campaigns. It was during this time when I worked with brands like Horizon Organic, Silk soymilk, GEICO insurance, A&E television, and Sobieski vodka.

Much of what we were doing at this time was totally new—it had never been tried before and we were learning and developing processes and policies as we went.

During this time, we were running a campaign to support a new soymilk product. We had collated a list of possible bloggers (we did not call them "online influencers" back then), who might want to test the product and write about it. We went through the normal research process that we always went through to find and identify the right bloggers—we researched, vetted, and selected bloggers based on the quality of their blog content, what we were outreaching for, and the audience they reached.

We had identified one blogger who seemed to align with the product and with our intended target audience. So we contacted him via email with our pitch.

And then it happened—what every social media marketer who works with online influencers fears—the blogger took our pitch email, posted it in its entirety on his blog, and annotated it, calling out everything we did wrong in the pitch email.

It turned out that while we had gone through our normal process, we had not read *enough* of his blog. These were the early days of working with these influencers, after all, so not a lot of best practices—or even just good practices—existed yet. And we missed an old post that he had written about soymilk a while before we reached out to him. It had been archived so it took some searching to find. But boy was it negative.

As a side note here, for those of you who are not aware, anti-soy communities are *huge* online. In short, the connection is to genetically modified organisms (GMOs). This community is large, well connected, and active. So when we inadvertently reached out to a blogger who happened to be "anti-soy" about promoting a soy product, well, let's just say we ignited a firestorm.

Our inexperience and our lack of preparation meant that we reached out to the wrong influencer. We jeopardized our client's reputation, and we ultimately lost a potential relationship that could have been established for other clients and future initiatives. And, of course, it also caused us some pretty substantial embarrassment.

I am not sharing this story with you to scare you—but really to emphasize what *not* to do. I learned a great lesson through this experience. It is crucial to be prepared when reaching out to influencers. Do your homework. Spend that little bit of extra time finding all those hidden posts. It will pay off in the long run by helping to avoid bigger issues.

Beginning Outreach

Once you have developed your list and vetted your influencers you can begin outreach. But even this requires a strategic approach—especially if you cannot pay them. Your first email should only gauge their interest—do not send tons of information and a full set of messages and assets. Consider how to pique their interest in learning more about your project in that initial email. You may want to offer to have a phone call to share the opportunity verbally, if that is something they would be interested in. After that initial contact—either via phone or follow-up email—only then should you share more information.

If you do not hear back from someone, that is okay. You can follow up. Keep in mind, these influencers are receiving numerous similar emails every day. Give them time to respond and do not take it personally if they do not respond right away. And do not worry about sending reminders. However, it is important not to pester and do not become contentious in your follow-up emails. This will not help the situation at all. I recommend that you do not send more than three outreach emails.

Conveying Your Messages

Once you have your campaigns developed, your goals set, and a set of influencers engaged, you will need to work with your influencers to find the right way to convey your messages to their followers. In Chapter 7, we will discuss influencer preferences for messages in more detail but it is worth touching on this subject here as well. Most influencers will have their own ideas for how to do this and it is vital that you be open to influencers' ideas. They know their audience the best, and they can really tell you what will work and what will not work with them.

However, some influencers may want your input and ideas. Many of the ones I have worked with over the years like to work collaboratively with me to develop the strategy. So you may need to share ideas for what influencers can do to support your initiatives. Below are some options to consider:

- Have them create video testimonials about your content
- Have them host or conduct a Facebook Live event, possibly interviewing an expert or other product representative
- Have them host contests or giveaways to engage their audiences, drive content development, and disseminate your product or message
- Have them cross-promote across platforms, as most social media influencers are active on more than one platform and will likely be willing to run a campaign on several different channels.

Final Reflections

In sum, it is important to consider these connections as relationships. Do not reach out *only* when you need something. Find ways to share information or opportunities with them that may be in their interest area but do not require them to write a post for you. Could you invite them to be a speaker at an event you are hosting? Is there a way for them to showcase their brand and expertise that they would benefit from? Are there initiatives you could include them in where they might get exposure to other brands with which they could build relationships?

These are not things you are asking them to do, but rather opportunities you are bringing to them. Create a two-way street of collaboration and make the relationship mutually beneficial.

So as you venture into this world of online influencers, consider, first, how times have changed—and how they continue to do so. Cooper's story evinces this—what was once an informal and organic community is now a highly organized and monetized industry. Even Heather Armstrong acknowledges this shift when she writes,

> Around the time of my divorce, mommy blogging turned into Influencer Marketing, and making a living as a professional blogger morphed into a shape that I did not recognize or sign up for. Manufacturing experiences for a brand and involving my children in those manufactured stories and photos stole a part of my soul that I have spent the last two years trying to get back.

While the introduction of money is a primary driver of these changes, the original tenets of connection, community, personal relevance, and compassion for others that drove Cooper to found The Motherhood still hold true today. And this is driving some influencers to build deeper relationships with each other and with issues that are important to them. But, even for this set of influencers, the networks they are creating may ultimately limit the sharing of new information, as they are often comprised solely of similar viewpoints, or as we have been calling them, "strong ties."

These factors are important to consider when identifying and reaching out to influencers about your particular initiative. You must understand the context in which you are asking them to support you. Moreover, you need to respect them and the process. Respect the things they want to write about. Respect their expertise on their topic. Respect their knowledge of their followers. Yes, you know your brand, your company, or your organization, but they know their community. This will, in turn, garner respect for your topic or issue. Respect that they are busy and that you need to plan around their editorial calendars. Respect that one outreach may not be enough, but 10 is likely too many.

At this point, we have dissected the industry of online influencers at length and I have given you some general heuristics to follow. But how do these things apply to the health context—because, after all, that is what we are all here for, right? This is the focus of the next chapter.

Chapter 4

Influencers and Health

health | /helTH/ | noun
The state of being free from illness or injury.

Over the course of my research, I had the opportunity to meet—and to hear the stories of—so many amazing influencers whose connections to health were uniquely their own. Below are three of their stories, each of which demonstrates a different pathway.

Monique's Story

The first time I met Monique was during the course of my research. She is an African American woman, a blogger, and a fitness enthusiast. When we met, she was 39 years old.

I only had the opportunity to speak with her a few times, but I will never forget her story.

A number of years before we met, her mother had passed away, and after her death, Monique struggled emotionally with the loss.

As a result, she gained a lot of weight. One day, a professor of hers called her "Precious" during a class. He was, of course, referring to the lead character in the 2009 movie, *Precious*, about a 16-year-old African American girl who was overweight.

Monique was devastated by this comment. Not only was she dealing with the death of her mother and struggling with her weight at this time, but now she had been publically humiliated by one of her professors. Someone who sat in a position of power and influence. Someone who should have supported her.

This was just too much for her to handle.

So she attempted suicide.

Fortunately, she was not successful.

As she went through her recovery, she began reflecting on this series of moments in her life. And she started to make some changes.

She started to work out. She was getting back in shape and losing weight. She started a fitness and health blog. And she joined a number of fitness and health influencer networks and connected with other influencer who were focused on the same topics she cared about.

What had once shattered her life, was now helping to shape a purpose for Monique. And that purpose was health.

Carol's Story

Carol is another influencer I met during the course of my research. An African American influencer, she writes about wine, Black hair, and other lifestyle-related topics. At the time when I met her, she was 44 years old.

While Monique's personal passion was health and fitness, Carol's was not. Unlike the focus of Monique's blog and social media content—which was health—Carol's blog is not, on its face, a natural fit for health content. So our conversations often focused on her relationship to health, how she saw it fitting into her blog and social media content (or not), and her perspectives on communicating about health issues to her followers.

When I first met Carol, her mom had just passed away. She had died from breast cancer. The death of her mother hit her hard. So hard, in fact, that she began to reexamine her own life and make changes to her health. She started eating healthier and taking better care of herself physically.

But when it came to her blog, she was not sure if and how to talk about it with her followers. She felt strongly that she needed to talk about her mother's passing, her struggle with breast cancer, and how these things had led her to take healthier steps in her own life. But she did not regularly touch on these kinds of topics on her blog. This was brand new territory for her.

She knew she had to approach the topic delicately and in a way that would fit with the rest of her content and be received well by her followers.

She decided to frame the post by starting with the story of her mother's struggle with breast cancer and her subsequent passing. But instead of ending the story there, she brought it back to the main focus of her blog—lifestyle.

She did this first by sharing the decisions she made about her own personal health as a result of her mother's death. She then further developed the piece into a larger discussion about health and nutrition in the African American community.

For Carol, an important part of any conversation about health was tying it to the larger context in which it is being discussed. Especially for influencers who do not regularly talk about health, this is paramount. And it should sound familiar—in Chapter 3, we talked about how influencers perceive themselves as brands and how the topics they choose to write about need to be related to that brand.

Regardless of the fact that Carol's blog did not naturally lend itself as a platform for conversations about health, she still felt that health had a place on her blog. In fact, she felt that health has a place on all blogs. It just had to be done in such a manner that it made sense. For her, talking about health meant talking about a lifestyle more broadly.

Sam's Story

I met Sam early in my career. I had worked with her on a number of campaigns and she had also participated in a number of studies I had conducted over the years. She is Caucasian and a scrapbooking-turned-lifestyle influencer. At the time when we were talking for my dissertation research, she was 49 years old.

Monique's and Carol's stories showcase the different approaches influencers may take to communicate about health issues that they are personally affected by.

But Sam's story is not that kind of story. Sam's story is about *not* being personally connected to a health issue but still finding the topic important to write about.

Sam's story starts years ago—before she became a blogger and an influencer.

As a working mom of two boys (who were aged 16 and 10, when we spoke), Sam was finding it increasingly challenging to balance work and home life, like so many other working moms. She certainly did not think that being a stay-at-home mom was easy, but doing both was becoming really difficult for her.

At the time, she has been working in auditing, and she had started a blog as a hobby. She loved scrapbooking and had started a blog about it, providing her followers with creative ideas, descriptions of how she did her scrapbooking projects, and overviews of different materials scrapbookers can use in their own projects.[56]

As she confronted her struggle to balance home and work life, she began to look for a new job that would allow her to have a better balance between the two. And in doing so, she started noticing all new types of opportunities related to social media and blogging. Years earlier, these had not existed, but now, she was learning that there were new ways for her to make a living and support her family doing this kind of work.

As a result of this, she decided to focus on developing her blog more. She worked on her content, writing more of it and promoting it more to increase her followership. And by doing this, she was eventually able to build up a revenue stream. She began to make enough money off her blog that she was able to work part time so that she could use the rest of her time to maintain and evolve her blog even more. Ultimately, this allowed her to both work and manage her blog while simultaneously achieving the work-life balance that she sought.

Then, around 2013, she started to evolve her blog content from just scrapbooking to talking about broader lifestyle topics. She started providing content geared toward women, not just scrapbookers, and she had a strong focus on content tailored to moms with older kids. She recognized, at the time, that this kind of focus for her blog could be somewhat limiting. It might not appeal to all readers. It could alienate others. But she felt strongly that this was her space on the web and doing this work had to make her happy, so she decided to really own this kind of content for this kind of audience.

When I asked her how she felt about writing about health topics, she responded that she likes to regularly write about health and wellness. She sees health is an important issue for everyone—in one form or another. Similar to Carol, she saw the topic of health as fitting more easily into a general lifestyle context. She also acknowledged that there were a lot of different types of topics under the health umbrella that her followers would be interested in. Things like eating better, getting more exercise, drinking more water, and taking vitamins all were topics that she could write about and that her followers would be find interesting.

While diet and exercise are fairly benign topics, Sam said that she also does not mind writing about more controversial topics like vaccination. Generally speaking, her approach to selecting health topics to write about is to remain open to all ideas—at least initially. She will not say "no" to a health-related initiative immediately. While some topics may be uncomfortable to write about (and she might ultimately say "no" after the idea is presented), to her, nothing is off-limits.

What is key to her decision to write (or not write) about a health issue, though, is the freedom to write about these topics in ways she sees appropriate for herself and for her followers.

For example, she once participated in an initiative about HPV vaccination. She decided to write about this topic—which, of course, can be incredibly controversial for some followers—because she felt that, despite the debate over vaccines and specifically the HPV vaccine, it was important information to share with her followers.

So she shared the information—factually and without emotion. And instead of receiving angry anti-vaccine comments, her followers responded really positively to the post. In fact, it was so impactful with followers that she still talks about this post with her family, friends, and even some of her followers today—years later.

This is the key for Sam. Giving her followers factual and accurate information and allowing them to make their own choices. This is the best way, for her, to talk about health issues that she sees as important, regardless of whether she has a personal connection to them or not. She does not push her beliefs about health on them. She does not "tell." She just simply shares. As she said,

> Everyone is free to make their own choice – that is what is beautiful about this country – but you need the information.

By approaching the many topics of health in this manner, regardless of whether she is personally connected to an issue or not, Sam can feel confident about writing about a wide variety of topics. In fact, her lack of personal connection to issues allows her to be more objective about them. And this style of writing appears to be received well by followers.

Monique's story demonstrates how some influencers are passionate about health from the get-go—and engaging them to support your issue may be easier than engaging influencers who are not already health advocates. Monique's blog was the result of various health-related personal experiences, and the things she writes about continue to be driven by her passion for the subject.

Carol's story, on the other hand, demonstrates how having a strong personal connection to a health issue can help make that issue relevant to influencers who do not talk about health on a regular basis. Carol's blog existed long before she cared about health as a blog topic, but now she finds ways to weave health messages into her blog content while still staying true to her original content focus.

Sam's story compliments Monique's and Carol's stories. For Sam, writing about health is considered a responsibility. She provides her followers with all the information and, then, lets them make the final decision about what is right for them.

Sam's story provides insight into how online influencers who may not be directly tied to an issue can still be motivated to write about it. Working with them, on their terms, to share information—and trusting them to share that information in a way that is effective with their followers—is key. In this way, Sam provides a great example of how to engage this type of influencer to support your issue.

Ultimately, how online influencers come to the topic of health is not universal and not necessarily linear. It is complex and oftentimes messy, but that messiness means that there is an opportunity. There is the potential to weave health into any context—if the story is a strong one and the influencer sees a place for it both in their writing and with their followers.

Understanding these varying kinds of perspectives from influencers about sharing health issues is important to ensure that you can accurately and successfully disseminate your health message. This will be the focus of the rest of this chapter.

Influencers Willingness to Talk About Health

Trying to understand someone's willingness to write about health is not a new idea. In fact, one's willingness to communicate about health—or any topic for that matter—is one that has been studied a lot.

In order to understand how influencers perceive communicating about health, it helps to start at the beginning and talk a little about individuals' willingness to communicate more generally.

The idea of one's willingness to communicate is really just about understanding whether someone is likely to approach or avoid starting a conversation.[57] Individuals are often more likely to communicate with others with whom they are close, and with whom they have frequent contact.[58]

This should sound familiar. We have discussed these same qualities at length in earlier chapters.

As it relates to health, research tells us that, generally speaking, the more one is willing to talk about health, the more knowledgeable they are about health. This, in turn, often determines their actual behaviors, with those who are more willing to talk about health also exhibiting healthier behaviors.[59] As well, it often signals how those whom we surround ourselves with feel about health, e.g., if I am a healthier person than it is likely that those around me will also be healthy, and vice versa.

But how does this translate into the online influencer context?

Well, as with communicating about heath more generally, the data suggest that influencers who choose to communicate about health can be incredibly persuasive with their audiences, and this, in turn, can alter people's health behaviors.

For example, in one study I worked on, we engaged mommy bloggers to share information about environmental risk factors for breast cancer with their followers. Upon evaluating the influence of these bloggers based on the perceptions of their followers, we discovered that blog followers who read and recalled this information were significantly more likely to share the breast cancer risk and prevention information they read than blog readers who did not see or recall the information. More importantly, however, we also learned that they were more likely to be open to receiving these messages in this format, to believe them to be accurate, and to take action to reduce breast cancer risk because the bloggers shared the information with them.[60]

As well, anecdotal evidence from other studies I have led further support this claim. For instance, Sam, the scrapbooking-turned-lifestyle influencer we met earlier, had this exact experience after writing her HPV vaccination blog post. One of her followers expressed her regret for missing out on an opportunity to vaccinate her sons for HPV, saying:

> Ok, I was literally JUST talking with my doctor yesterday about this. He was SUPER neutral about if my boys should get them or not. So we left without getting them, now I am regretting it.[61]

Thus, we can see that online influencers have the ability to shift knowledge, attitudes, and possibly even behaviors related to health among their followers. But why is this?

You may recall from Chapter 2 that the influence of opinion leaders—both online and offline—extends from their credibility with others. Well, online influencer credibility with their followers plays the same function as it relates to health. As Susan, a 30-year-old Asian healthy living and lifestyle influencer, said,

> I think many [followers] trust that I do the research beforehand, and when I talk about a certain health subject, they are more compelled to listen as I believe they see me as a somewhat credible source.

But in order to affect this kind of change, you first have to get online influencers to talk about your health topics. And in order to understand how influencers choose the topics they talk about, we need to first understand the factors that they take into consideration when making these types of decisions about content.

A primary driver of this decision-making process has to do whether they think their followers want to receive health information from them. And, it turns out that, yes, most influencers who participated in my research think that their followers do want to receive health information from them.

Moreover, at this point in the book, we have seen evidence of this as well. The findings from the environmental risk breast cancer study mentioned above demonstrate this. As well, Sam's story emphasizes this point well because she understood what kinds of health information her followers want and the format in which they want to receive that information.

However, while followers are receptive to reading about health topics on blogs, it does not mean that they are open to reading about *all* health topics. In fact, findings from my research suggest that influencers who do not think their followers will want to read about a particular topic will often choose not to write about it, regardless of whether they personally think it is important information to share.

We saw this exemplified in Elle's story from earlier, where she described how she chooses to write only about certain topics on her blog (and keep her other interests private) because she knows her followers do not want to see that kind of content.

As well, Ingrid, a 34-year-old Asian mommy and lifestyle influencer I met during the course of my research, shared that she picks topics that are good for her reputation with her followers. She does not want to invite controversy or negative comments on her blog so she steers clear of issues that may do that. Further, she says that by carefully selecting health topics tailored to her followers' interests, she solidifies her role as an opinion leader for her them. They know they will not get something that they do not want to read or hear about and as such, trust that Ingrid has their best interests at heart when she writes about something.

What is interesting about this is that Ingrid is a nurse so she knows the value of health information—and of writing about it. Despite this, however, she chooses to write only about select topics. For instance, she has done posts about medication use during pregnancy, and cold- and flu-related topics. For her, her followers' needs trump the importance of the health issue—if they will not read it or will react negatively to it, she will not share it.

Another consideration for influencers when deciding to write about health topics has to do with how they perceive their blog or social media. Health topics can be serious, but often, influencers see their blog or social media as their "happy place" and as places for fun and lighthearted content. As Molly, a 38-year-old Caucasian sexual health influencer I met, said,

> My blog is kind of like my happy place.

This limits, then, how much "serious stuff" they may want to write about. So despite the fact that influencers like Carol and Sam choose to write about health, not all will do this. As noted previously, even Sam, the 49-year-old Caucasian lifestyle influencer who said that no health topic is off-limits, said,

> It's my space on the web so it has to make me happy.

Ultimately, influencers' willingness to communicate about health can be powerful—we know now that it can shape perceptions and possibly change behavior. However, influencers' decisions about whether to communicate or not about a health topic are deeply connected to their personal perspectives about what their followers want to maintaining their credibility with them, and to whether a health topic aligns (or doesn't) with their own perspectives of their blog or social media.

This suggests that there could be some challenges with influencers' willingness to communicate about health. We will discuss these in the next section.

Challenges with Influencers' Willingness to Communicate About Health

As we have been discussing, many influencers, regardless of the topic, try and provide unique content for their followers.

Moreover, the content that is selected and the ways in which it is written is often imbued "with a strong sense of the author's personality, passions, and point of view."[62–64] You can see this exemplified in the stories of Ingrid, Sam, Carol, and Elle that we have been discussing thus far.

As well, Theresa, a 39-year-old African American mommy influencer I met, said,

> [I write about issues that are] more from the perspective of issues that affect people I know in real life. It's easier to take information from someone who has been there in the trenches.

Yet, while this personal narrative approach can help instill them with credibility, this style also poses a number of challenges to communicators.

First, as we discussed earlier, influencers' personal point of view can lead them to write about topics in ways that are problematic for their followers, such as providing outdated or impractical information. They may also only write about part of the story—not necessarily because they want to, but rather, it just may be that they do not have all the information.

Additionally, inaccurate messaging can lead to the conveyance of misinformation or endorsement of products or beliefs that may not be helpful to followers (and could, in fact, be harmful). Moreover, without new and different information being shared, such misinformation will continue to circulate and may become perceived as true, ultimately normalizing that information among an audience group.

For health, this has important, and real-life, implications. As Risk and Petersen state,

> A plethora of inaccurate and even potentially life-threatening content readily accessible to anyone with a modem and an Internet browser supports the validity of that concern. For instance, Crocco, Villasis-Keever and Jadad (2002) reported that inaccurate Internet information contributed to harm in a 1-year-old boy with diarrhea.[65]
>
> (p. 2713)

Perhaps no other health topic exemplifies this more than that of vaccination. Vaccination is one of the most well-known topics where online influencers have, for decades, shared false and unfounded information. Moverover, the fact that the health world joined the conversation much later (arguably, too late) allowed anti-vaccinators to spread false information widely, ultimately shifting perceptions and beliefs about vaccination that still endure today.

Finally, these issues are only exacerbated by this trend of influencers coalescing around strong tie relationships (again, those individuals who are like-minded), as we discussed in the last chapter. This limits the amount of new information that can be introduced between people and therefore serves to just perpetuate these issues of limited, inaccurate, or misinformation.

To overcome such barriers, it is my belief that health communicators need to be engaging with influencers to introduce such new information to them and their followers. We cannot always change how influencers coalesce online and as the industry shifts, common interests, rather than diverse ones, are bringing influencers together. But as individuals who come from a different background and do not necessarily spend a lot of time in this influencer industry, we can be the "weak ties" needs to introduce such new information.

Therefore, both types of "ties" have important roles to play in communicating health information. First, the "strong ties," or the online influencers, are needed in order to credibly transmit health information to their audiences. But the health experts, or the "weak ties," are incredibly important for introducing such new—and accurate—information. Ultimately, as it relates to communicating about health, "weak ties" and "strong ties" must work collaboratively to achieve positive health outcomes vis-à-vis these online influencers.

A final barrier to influencers writing about health that I uncovered in my research was simply that many influencers had not yet really thought much about how health could fit into their existing content. As Maria, a 44-year-old Hispanic mommy and travel influencer I met, said,

> Health is huge, and it is something everyone deals with. [This conversation] made me think about how to integrate health into my [content].

And Maria's perspective is not unique. Travel influencers are one subgroup of influencers where health is often not discussed. Traditionally, travel influencers have seen their role as promoting coveted travel experiences by showcasing beautiful photos, exotic locations, and exciting adventures.

Despite health being a serious topic, which may seem at odds with this image, there is actually a really important place in this conversation for health messaging. Travelers face a plethora of potential health issues and are often required to get certain vaccines and tests done in advance of or upon returning from a trip, depending on where they are going. Sharing this information, while perhaps scary to some, seems like it would be really important to share. Thus, these influencers have the potential to be a very important conduit for health information that is relevant to their followers who may be traveling to areas that have health issues that they need to be aware of and take precautions against.

This finding made me think that there may be some confusion about how influencers from all walks of life can think about integrating health content into their blog or social media. For example, if you are a crafting influencer,

Table 4.1 Possible Health Topic by Influencer Type

Influencer Type	*Possible Health Topics*
Overall health	Nutrition; physical activity; stress management; integrative heath practices; aging; other related health issues
Parenting	Child development; healthy pregnancy; stress management; unexpected pregnancy; disabilities awareness; vaccinations; aging; other related health issues
Pregnancy	Healthy pregnancy; unexpected pregnancy; asthma; diabetes prevention and management; disabilities awareness; vaccinations; heart health; blood disorders; stress management; aging; other related health issues
Sexual wellness	Sexual health; healthy pregnancy; unexpected pregnancy; HIV/AIDS prevention and testing; aging
Nutrition	Nutrition; physical activity; integrative heath practices; asthma; diabetes prevention and management; aging; other related health issues
Fitness	Physical activity; nutrition; asthma; diabetes prevention and management; stress management; integrative heath practices; aging; other related health issues
Calligraphy	Arthritis prevention and treatment; aging; eye health; other related health issues

(*Continued*)

Table 4.1 (*Continued*) Possible Health Topic by Influencer Type

Influencer Type	*Possible Health Topics*
Quilting	Arthritis prevention and treatment; aging; eye health; other related health issues
New age/Yoga/non-traditional/ Eastern medicine	Integrative heath practices; nutrition; stress management; mental health; other related health issues
Travel	Infectious diseases; sexual health; vaccinations; area-specific outbreaks; other related health issues
Recipe/food	Diabetes prevention and management; nutrition; physical activity; other related health issues
Movies/television/books/ pop-culture	Health topics that are being covered in the media; health issues that are tied to current pop culture and celebrity; other related health issues
Mattress	Safe sleep; sleep disorders; co-sleeping; other related health issues
Gardening	Nutrition; physical activity; aging; arthritis; asthma; diabetes prevention and management; allergies; other related health issues
Beauty/fashion	Health as part of beauty; nutrition; physical activity; safe weight; aging; HIV testing; sexual health; asthma; diabetes prevention and management; other related health issues

(*Continued*)

Table 4.1 (*Continued*) Possible Health Topic by Influencer Type

Influencer Type	*Possible Health Topics*
Money	Money as part of overall health; nutrition; physical activity; heart health; stress management; other related health issues
Outdoor enthusiast/survival	Nutrition; physical activity; heart health; stress management; clean water; asthma; trauma prevention and management; allergies; other related health issues
Organization	Workplace health; nutrition; physical activity; vaccinations
Tech	Nutrition; physical activity; heart health; asthma; diabetes prevention and management; workplace health; other related health issues
Sports	Nutrition; physical activity; head injury safety; asthma; trauma prevention, treatment, and management
Home décor	Health as part of design; nutrition; physical activity; aging; arthritis; other related health issues
Religious/spiritual	Health as part of spirituality; heart health; nutrition; mental health; physical activity
Political	Health policy; advocacy; health topics currently being covered in the media

it may not clear to you where health can fit into your daily posts. To help clarify how I perceive health fitting into everyday conversations, Table 4.1 maps a variety of health topics to a variety of influencer topics areas.

Ultimately, finding ways to introduce health as a topic into places where it might not otherwise be discussed is critical to ensuring that we are infusing existing conversations with new information about health. We need to have a mix of "strong ties" and "weak ties" to make this work. Moreover, while many influencers are willing to talk about health, you may need to work with them to figure out which topics are a fit and which ones are not.

Final Reflections

Thus far, we have talked at length about how health, and writing about it, is risky for online influencers.

And throughout this discussion, it has become clear that at the root of making decisions about communicating about health are influencers' perceptions of risk. To better understand these perceptions, some further discussion of risk and risk perceptions is warranted. This will be the focus of the next chapter.

Chapter 5

Perceptions of Risk

risk | /risk/ | noun
A situation involving exposure to danger.

A couple of years ago, on behalf of a well-known national health organization working to educate the public about the importance of vaccines, a group of online influencers was engaged to host an hour-long Twitter chat on childhood vaccinations.[66] The chat was intended to share reputable information and resources about vaccines and engage parents and caregivers on the topic of vaccination for their families.

It was suspected that this topic would be particularly divisive because, as we have been discussing, there are strong opinions and intense conversations about vaccination online. There have been for years. For example, an analysis of vaccine-related Google searches found that the majority of the top Google search results contained anti-vaccination sentiments.[67] As well, an analysis of vaccination videos on YouTube found that those with an anti-vaccination message had higher ratings and more views than pro-vaccine videos.[68]

Given this, the chat organizers knew they needed to be prepared for something to go wrong.

And indeed it did. Leading up to the chat, a group of anti-vaccination influencers found out about it and starting tweeting using the chat hashtag (#CDCvax) trying to sway people either not to participate at all or to get their followers to show up to the chat in order to disrupt it.

And their pre-promotion worked. The day of the chat, they did show up. They actively participated in the chat sharing alternative resources and disrupting the conversation. The one-hour chat felt like it lasted an eternity. The chat organizers were managing their own messages as well as those from the anti-vaccine community. It was rough.

But the organizers had been prepared. That morning, knowing that it would be a "lively" chat, to say the least, the chat organizers met to discuss what to do. They knew they could cancel the chat, but that did not seem like a very effective strategy to use—at the end of the day, these messages were really important to share and they were not going to be bullied into not sharing them.

They also knew they were going to need a strategy to be able to deal with these kinds of counter-messages. The chat organizers had already engaged a number of influencers to help host the event, and these ended up being their best asset. The organizers enlisted the hosts to help repudiate these messages, doing so by creating a counter-promotion strategy to engage their followers to join the chat and help balance the conversation.

So yes, the anti-vaccine community did show up, and yes, the chat was lively. A review of the chat's metrics showed there was a 1,176 percent increase in the number of people talking about the topic, when conversation levels before the chat were compared with those during the chat.

But the organizers' preparation paid off. Further, the top ten highest-reaching anti-vaccine advocates had a total of 44,307 followers (an average of around 4,400 followers per person). Yet, the top ten pro-vaccine advocates had a combined following of 175,678 (or an average of around 17,500 followers per person). Thus, the reach of the anti-vaccine advocates was dwarfed by that of the pro-vaccine advocates.

Moreover, while approximately 17 percent of the tweets shared during the chat were negatively valenced toward vaccination, those tweets generated fewer than 3 percent of the overall chat impressions. Therefore, while the anti-vaccine sentiment may have felt overwhelming during the chat, when we reviewed the data, they really only represented a small fraction of the conversation.

Of course, the lightening rod that is vaccination is nothing new to online audiences. It has been a hot topic for influencers for years. And as a result, anytime there is a conversation about vaccination in social media, there is a risk that anti-vaccine advocates will organize to join the conversation and disrupt it.

Vaccination, as a risk-laden topic, does not just mean having to deal with anti-vaccine comments during a chat or other live event; rather, it also means having to deal with negative comments on one's own blog or social media profile and the fear that an influencer's own platform could be co-opted to share false information vis a vis those negative comments.

This was Melody's experience.

Melody is an influencer I met a couple of years ago. At the time, she had been commissioned by a national pharmacy to write a post about flu season to promote the flu vaccine.[69] In response, she received a large number of anti-vaccination comments from her followers. She was not surprised that this happened. Nor was she bothered by it. She had often had these kinds of experiences when she wrote about controversial issues, such as vaccination on her blog.

What she *was* bothered by was the negative tone of the comments on her blog and the "name calling" that ensued.

Moreover, she was bothered by what she referred to as the "false arguments" that were being perpetuated—and that her blog was being used to perpetuate them. She worried about her blog being used as a channel for misinformation.

This experience really made her reevaluate whether writing about vaccination was worth it—even though she was strongly pro-vaccine. She said,

> I really don't think we're changing people's minds that aren't willing to vaccinate, so it just depends on if I am in the mood to deal with the responses… They go to their natural news or their website and copy and paste a whole bunch of stuff into a comment. Then if I delete a comment I am called closed-minded.

There was a real risk for her in sharing this kind of information, even if it was evidence-based and even if she did believe in the accuracy and importance of it. These negative comments posed a number of challenges for her. First, the inaccuracy of the comments some people left on her blog meant that false information was being shared with her followers. As well, the name-calling that ensued meant that her platform was also being used to bully and disparage her and her followers. Finally, all of this discussion that was happening would now be associated with her brand because it was all happening on her platform.

But influencer concerns about risk and talking about risky topics are not just relegated to health topics. You can see this kind of thing play out similarly with any number of topics. For example, in 2018, Emily Henderson, who writes the blog, Style by Emily Henderson, Instagrammed a post about former President Obama, writing,

> Tired on a Saturday night. Remembering a man who actually cared about the future of women. This man.

> [heart emoji] (I don't know if his T-shirt is photoshopped but I know, believe and love his general feminist message that can not be faked. Double tap if you agree with it).[70]

In response to this post, she received almost 2,500 comments, many of which were negative. She also lost 4,000 followers—*in just one night.*

While she had not known it before, this experience really crystallized for her that most of her audience follows her *only* for one type of content. The type of content that she became known for and built her brand on. Her design-related content.

So when she posted something not related to design, something that was off-brand, the post did not resonate well with all of them. In short, she realized that they wanted her to stay in her lane and "stick to design."[71]

The stories of Melody and Emily as well as the vaccination chat story demonstrate how risk is closely interwoven with the content, brands, and experiences that influencers have created for themselves—and others—online. As a result, many of them tend to be risk averse, wanting to generally avoid controversy and not do anything that will evoke negative reactions from their followers.

There is risk for influencers in selecting the topics they choose to write about. There is risk in sharing something they feel passionate about, knowing that it could alienate some members of their audience. There is also risk that misinformation will be spread. And there is risk that this can tarnish a brand irreparably.

For health, which is private, personal, and often stigmatized, the risks can be even more polarizing and can have larger ramifications. Therefore, understanding risk and influencers' perceptions of risk are important aspects of working with them. As well, risk is not just a concern for influencers, but it is also a concern for brands and organizations. These topics are the focus of the rest of the chapter.

What Is Risk?

Risk is defined as "the probability that an event will occur."[72] Risk pertains to increasing or decreasing necessary causes, which are the exposures that always precede a particular outcome.

In terms of social media, risk often is a major consideration due to the open nature of the medium and how active and vocal people can be online. In fact, Pekka Aula writes in his article, "Social media, reputation risk and ambient publicity management," that

> Reputation risk, the possibility or danger of losing one's reputation, presents a threat to competitiveness, positioning, the trust and loyalty of stakeholders, media relations, the legitimacy of operations, and even the license to exist.

The fact that influencers see themselves as brands means that they care about the things that pose threats to their positioning in the marketplace, their competitiveness against other influencers, the trust and loyalty of their followers, the networks they belong to, their sponsors and partners, and their credibility. This means they want to—and need to—maintain their relationships with sponsors and to do this, they need to keep their followers coming back.

Thus, risk is real for influencers. If they say or do something that alienates their followers, their reputation could be jeopardized and they could lose followers, paid engagements, and ultimately income. So weighing the risk of sharing information about health (or any other topic) will be an important part of the decision-making process about whether or not to work with an initiative.

How We Process Risk

It may appear that online influencers will make decisions about risk simply by thinking, "Well, the topic of vaccination is risky, and it'll invite controversy so I will not write about it." But how influencers—and people more generally—process risk is not that simple.

When we process the risk of doing something, two cognitive processes occur. First, we assess the threat, and second, we assess our ability to respond to that threat.[73] Therefore, such risky situations are assessed from a problem-solution orientation.[74]

Within each of these two processes, there are two considerations that humans take into account. As it relates to our assessment of the threat, we assess our own susceptibility to the threat, which means that we assess how likely the threat is to impact us.[75] As well, we assess the severity of the threat, which refers our assessment of the magnitude of the threat, were we to be affected.

As it relates to our ability to respond to the threat, we consider our own sense of self-efficacy, or our own assessment of whether we are competent to perform the tasks needed to control the risk. As well, we assess our response efficacy, or whether we think the actions we think we can take to control the threat will, if employed, successfully control the threat.

It is through these processes that we are both assessing the risk as well as our ability to mitigate that risk in order to make decisions about things in our lives.

Influencer Perceptions of Risk

So far, we have been discussing how influencers consider themselves to be brands and how this is connected to their willingness to communicate about health. We have also established that the act of discussing health issues on their blog or social media can be risky for influencers—especially if they are talking about controversial topics.

But how online influencers make decisions about the risk of communicating about health is not necessarily a simple or straightforward process. Therefore, the problem-solution orientation we just discussed can be used to better understand how they may process this kind of risk.

Let's consider, first, the problem dimension of the orientation. Within this dimension, a primary consideration for influencers is dealing with the health issue itself. Specifically, they will need to assess their or their followers' susceptibility to the health issue. They also need to evaluate how severe the health issue really is, were they and/or their followers to be affected.

A second consideration within the problem dimension, however, has to do with the risk of *communicating* about the health issue. For instance, influencers may weigh whether writing about a health issue will result in backlash from their community, and if so, they may assess how severe that backlash will be in order to determine if they will write about it.

Likewise, if we consider the solution dimension of the orientation, influencers may process risk on both the health issue and the health communication aspects of this dimension. To the first, they may assess whether they and/or their followers have the self-efficacy to be able to address the health issue, e.g., whether they are able to take the necessary actions to alleviate the issue. As well, influencers may consider whether taking those actions will work in successfully alleviating the issue.

As it relates to communicating about the issue, they may weigh whether writing about the health issue—and thereby sharing the actions required to alleviate the issue—will help increase this ability of their followers to respond successfully to the issue. As well, they may assess whether writing about these response actions will result in followers taking action and successfully addressing the issue.

Ok, yes. That was a lot. And it was also a very theoretical assessment of how an influencer may make a decision to write about a health topic. But how does this play out in real life? What does the evidence tell us? Well, findings from my research suggest that influencers do, in fact, process risk from a problem-solution orientation for both the health topic itself and the communication of that health topic.

As it relates to influencers' assessment of health risk, personal relevancy plays an important role. In short, influencers consider whether an issue affects them or someone they know and if so, how serious it really is.

The stories we heard from Monique and Carol in Chapter 4 exemplify how being personally affected by a health issue and experiencing the severity of it firsthand are compelling factors in how an influencer assesses their own risk or the potential risk to others who are like them. For example, Carol's experience with breast cancer not only meant that she understood that she or others in the African American community could be affected (susceptibility), but her mother's death made the seriousness of the issue salient (severity). Moreover, while she could not be sure whether changing her lifestyle would make a difference (response efficacy), she knew that changing her diet was something she could do that could help reduce her risk (self-efficacy).

As it relates to the risk of communicating about the health issue, the topic in question plays a major role. Some health topics are generally perceived to be less controversial. These include issues such as child development, nutrition, physical activity, healthy pregnancy, diabetes, heart disease, and cancer.

When the focus of a health initiative is on one of these topics, influencers may decide to write about it because doing so may not result in much, if any, substantial backlash from their community (susceptibility and severity). As well, they may assess that by writing about it they will help their followers manage the issue successfully (self- and response efficacy).

However, the assessment process may be different if the issues are more controversial—and generally speaking, topics such as vaccination, sex and sexuality, gender issues, condom use, and infertility are ones that influencers are less willing to talk about. For instance, Emma, a 35-year-old Hispanic entertainment and technology influencer I met, said,

> We keep it very 'G[-rated on the blog]'.

As well, Miriam, the 30-year-old Asian health living and parenting influencer I met during the course of my research, said,

> I have mixed feelings [about]... topics where people have strong opinions.

Finally, Eric, a 36-year-old Caucasian Do-it-Yourself (DIY), parenting, and travel influencer I met during the course of my research, said,

> I won't write about controversial stuff like politics, religion, and sexual preferences.

Even Sue, a 30-year-old Asian mommy influencer I met, spelled out the word, "S. E. X.," during the course of our interview to reference a topic she would not write about on her blog.

In the case of these types of health issues, influencers may assess the risk and intensity of follower backlash as something they do not want to deal with (susceptibility and severity). As well, if they do not think their followers will be receptive to information on these topics, then they may not view writing about it as helping their followers deal successfully with the issue (self- and response efficacy).

Thus, a main contributing factor in an influencer's assessment of the risk of communicating about a health issue is the quality and tone of follower comments. Influencers who are less comfortable with dealing with negative comments often avoid talking about a health topic that will invite these kinds of comments. As Miriam, the 30-year-old Asian healthy living and parenting influencer, said,

> I am very into natural healing, and although I do write about different natural remedies, I understand that many people will not agree with me,

> so I oftentimes keep a lot of my information to myself to avoid people being judgmental about it.

As well, Laura, a 34-year-old multiracial recipe influencer, said,

> I get a little nervous about sharing my story [because] I'm not sure how they will handle the information or what questions will be asked ... Comments can be scary. But I keep reminding myself that people are going through this and it's important to share my story. This is all they know and the examples they see are not always representative, so I want to be that voice. I do it for them. There are people looking for the information.

As well, Melody's story (that we started this chapter with) exemplifies this struggle with being supportive of a health issue but refusing to communicate about it due to the risk involved.

Specifically, vaccination was noted numerous times throughout my research as a health topic that influencers are wary to write about, regardless of their personal feelings about vaccination. Miriam, the 30-year-old Asian healthy living and parenting influencer, said,

> I have mixed feelings about vaccinations and avoid writing about them because of possible backlash from my readers.

Like Melody, many influencers felt fatigued by the anti-vaccine community, such that many influencers—even if they supported vaccination—reported being unwilling to write about it on their blog or social media. Dealing with negative follower comments in relation to vaccination was just too much for them to deal with.

But it is also not just about the negative comments. In some cases, it may be about an influencer's ability to manage questions from their followers about the health topics they write about. Generally speaking, if influencers feel that they are unable to successfully manage such questions, they may be less inclined to write about a health issue. As many of them are not trained medical professionals, they worry that they will not be able to properly advise their followers if there are questions about what they have written. As Melanie, a 39-year-old Hispanic mommy, lifestyle, and travel influencer I met, said,

> [Influencers need to be] super careful about health advising, we are not doctors, I would urge them to ask their questions to a [health care professional].

Moreover, as we have been seeing, there is not just one way or reason that influencers decide to write (or not write) about health. Despite how an influencer might traditionally assess the risk of writing about a topic—especially if it is controversial—they may still be willing to write about it. And not all influencers worry about follower comments. As Leah, a 29-year-old African American lifestyle influencer who was very comfortable with negative feedback, said,

> I'm comfortable. I want them to come to me. I am open to negative comments. I see it as, we all come from different walks of life. I am open to that dialogue.

One reason for this is altruism. In this case, even despite the risk and severity of follower backlash, if an influencer feels that sharing information on his or her blog or social media will help someone, he/she may be more inclined to do so. For instance, Sara, a 54-year-old Caucasian mom influencer I met during the course of my research, said,

> I have to believe in and stand behind the idea and/or product in order to endorse it or write about it. If I feel strongly about a certain health subject, I will absolutely be motivated to write about it!

As well, Sarah, a Hispanic mommy, lifestyle, and travel influencer I met, said,

> Topics that benefit others [would motivate me to share health information with my readers].

Laura, the 34-year-old multiracial recipe influencer I met, also said,

> I try to be a voice for those that don't have a voice ... my family knows I will talk about most anything. I want to help others understand what's going on and be there if someone has questions.

Finally, Leah, a 29-year-old African American lifestyle influencer I met, said,

> You don't need to sacrifice something to focus on something else. I want to inspire [my readers] to take that back and do what is best for [them].

As well, the personal relevancy of a health topic that we discussed earlier may also lead influencers to write about the topic. This is because they have experienced the issue and how bad it can be, and they know by sharing actionable information via their blog or social media, they might help their followers successfully deal with the issue.

So here is how I would sum all of this up. Influencers may decide to write (or not write) about a topic for any number of reasons—if they think the issue affects or does not affect them or their followers, if they consider it too severe or not severe enough, if they feel that it will invite too much negativity, or if they feel that writing about it will help their followers. But personal connection to an issue and good old fashioned altriusm can really sway an influencer's perception of risk and ultimately their decision to communicate about health.

Finally, risk perceptions can shift over time so there may always be an opportunity to work with someone who initially is more risk averse. As Leah, a 29-year-old African American lifestyle influencer I met, said,

> I am more comfortable now than I was in the beginning. [Now] I want to get myself uncomfortable and show those dirty parts.

At this point, we have a good sense of how influencers may process risk. Clearly topics and follower feedback are factors in their decision-making process. And while some influencers will never talk about certain health issues, not all influencers process risk this same way. This means there are still opportunities for these influencers and health communicators to work together.

However, the risk is not only for the influencers. It is also for the health initiatives that work with them. We will tackle this next.

Risk for Brands and Organizations

We have talked at length about risk as it pertains to online influencers, but this is not the only type of risk that is involved when working with online influencers.

A very important aspect of risk to consider is risk for the organization. As noted above, Pekka Aula says that reputation—and the risk of losing that reputation—is a sizeable threat, and he notes that this is particularly true for organizations.

Because of this, organizations and brands, which are developing and implementing initiatives with influencers must ensure that they work with the right kind of influencers and trusted networks. It also means that they must do their homework before embarking on a project with any influencer.

We discussed in Chapter 3 strategies for identifying and building relationships with influencers that can help ensure that your message is disseminated accurately and the way you intend. As it relates to risk, the same holds true. Working with online influencers—and the networks that manage them—with whom you have built strong relationships will help ensure that your goals are achieved and that risks are minimized.

Having these strong, vetted relationships in place allows you to cherry pick influencers in order to ensure that the right messenger can take your message to the right audience in the right way.

It also allows you to quickly activate influencers if there is a timely message that needs to get out. For example, if there is an outbreak or if new data about a particular topic is being released, having these relationships at your fingertips can ensure that your message gets to the people who need it most in a timely manner.

Finally, it ensures that you are not scrambling at the last minute to find influencers to share your message, that you give yourself enough time to properly vet them, and that you don't run the risk of engaging someone who will "go rogue" and post off-message. Moreover, if something is misstated or factually incorrect, having these relationships allows you to go back to the influencer and ask for a correction to be made, thus ensuring the accuracy of the message.

We briefly talked about messaging in Chapter 3 and we will devote a whole chapter to it when we get to Chapter 7, but it is worth some discussion here as well because messaging is an important aspect of reducing a brand or organization's risk.

And this is where the importance of developing a clear and accurate messaging document comes in to play. A messaging document lays out all the points that you want the influencer to convey. It also provides important links and graphics, as well as draft or example social media posts that the influencers can easily use in social media.

The messaging document is also important because it helps ensure that the most important messages are captured and highlighted for the influencer making it easy for them to post the right message. This helps avoid the issue of false or misinformation being shared.

The messaging document is meant to be a guide for your influencers though. They may take the content as is, but they may also choose to edit it for their platform. Best practices suggest that you should not request to review their posts—and especially not to edit them. The social channels and blogs that they write on are their platforms written in their voices and from their perspective. And really, this is what makes disseminating information via influencers special. It is your information conveyed in a way that readers and followers will understand and be receptive to. And if you edit them, it is really not *from them*.

You can, of course, go back and request a small edit or two if there is something inaccurate, but as a general rule of thumb, you should have prepared the influencer well enough that they can write their posts on-message the first time, while still maintaining their own voice.

Paying for a post can give you a little more leeway to ask for review and approval of the final content, but it is still not recommended. But if you are not paying for a post, then you really should not ask to review the content. If an online influencer agrees to help you without payment, he/she is supporting you pro bono, and you should let them tell the story as they would and make it as easy as possible for them.

As well, it can happen—and I often see this in health-related initiatives—that influencers may proactively share a post with the organization or brand commissioning the post ahead of time to ensure that the message is correct. With health, the best influencers really care about what they are writing and want to make sure that they are not giving their followers the wrong information.

Two final points that are related to organization or brand risk include the development of an escalation policy and the power of community in dealing with risk. I elaborate on both of these below.

To the first point—the development of an escalation policy—every good social media strategist should have developed one of these for their initiative, organization, or brand. An escalation plan documents processes and approaches for dealing with people online in social media—both the good and the bad. Dealing with the good stuff may seem easy but it is still worth documenting. This means documenting approaches for thanking social media users who comment positively on a post as well as the process for sharing or liking an influencer post that you have commissioned. While simple, these things should be discussed internally at your organizations as they may raise questions about perceived endorsement or partnership, and depending on the industry, there may be limitations to what you are allowed to do. So spend some time thinking about how to deal with the good stuff.

Once you have the good stuff figured out, you can turn your attention to dealing with the bad.

Dealing with the bad means having a plan for how to address an issue that has arisen publicly. In social media, these decisions need to be made quickly so that the issue can be dealt with before it becomes something bigger.

In order to be able to do this, your escalation plan should document the processes and policies for dealing with these issues ahead of time, so when something does go wrong, you do not need to figure it out in that moment. You should consider things like:

- What happened? Did a blogger go rogue and publicly diverge from your messages or did an on-message blog post cause a firestorm of negative off-message comments from followers?
- How will you handle these scenarios? Will you respond publically or try and let it die down on it's own?
- Who are the key decision-makers who need to be at the table when something goes wrong to decide how to respond and/or approve a public response?

These are things you should plan for ahead of time in order to be able to deal with them swiftly if—and when—they happen.

Finally—to the second point about the power of community—when you have an engaged and trusted network of supporters, they can often be your best advocates when something goes wrong. But this is based on trust, and that trust comes from knowing them, working with them, and entrusting them with your message. Only then do they feel that they are part of the initiative, that they have a stake in it, and can own it—regardless of what happens.

The opening story for this chapter about the chat exemplifies both of these final best practices for brands. You will recall that during a vaccine-related chat, a group of anti-vaccination advocates showed up with the aim of disrupting the conversation. However, the team managing the chat was so well prepared with their messaging and escalation plan that when the anti-vaccination advocates shows up in the chat, they were able to manage the lively discussion and negative content that was being posted. As well, because a group of mom bloggers had been engaged to help host the chat, they could come to the defense of the topic when the anti-vaccine community began their attack. And they were able to mobilize their own networks to help drown out the anti-vaccine messages.

Ultimately, the topic of health presents important risks for marketers, communicators, businesses, and brands. Considering these risks when planning your influencer outreach program—and reaching out to them—is key. As a marketer, communicator, organization, or brand, you need to be aware of how influencers perceive certain health topics and how comfortable they are with taking risks with their followers. This will help you identify the right influencers to work with and successfully engage them.

You also need to be honest with yourself about how much risk you are comfortable with. Perhaps working with influencers presents too much risk—and that is ok. The best situation is for you to be aptly prepared and ready to engage in this space, knowing you have your safety nets in place and are prepared to handle anything that comes your way.

And sometimes that means not engaging.

Final Reflections

We have covered risk at length—both for marketers and influencers alike. We know that brands are taking huge risks when working with influencers. But we also know that sometimes influencers just will not take the risk if they feel that the outcomes are not worth it for them.

Sometimes, however, influencers are willing to take that risk regardless of the outcomes. And this is despite huge obstacles that they might be facing. They do this because, regardless of these, they think they can make a difference. But why? What is going on when they do this? What drives them? Understanding this a bit better is the focus of the next chapter.

Chapter 6

It Is Just the Great Unknown—Or Is It?

> fa·tal·ism | /ˈfādlˌizəm/ | noun
> The belief that all events are predetermined and therefore inevitable.

We have been talking about health and risk—and how sometimes, just sometimes—influencers are willing to take risks regardless of the outcomes.

But how can this be when we know how risk averse influencers are?

Understanding this is our goal for this Chapter. But to situate this discussion, I want to tell you about two such influencers—Laura and Lisa. Their stories are below.

Laura's story

I met Laura during the course of my research. She is an influencer who writes about food, recipes, and health.

At the time when I met her, she was 34 years old.

Like so many other influencers I have met, Laura started her blog as a place to house family recipes and maintain personal connections. But over time, her audience grew. As she posted more content, more people began to follow her. Until finally, she was no longer writing for just her family, but for a larger, more diverse audience.

Yet, while her content broadened slightly to include more types of content than just recipes, she always kept it focused on food and health. This was her passion.

And this passion arose from her own personal struggles with health.

Laura suffers from spastic cerebral palsy, which is where the muscles feel stiff and movements may look mechanical and jerky. This can make movement difficult or even impossible. Laura also suffers from endometriosis, which is an often painful disorder in which tissue that normally lines the inside of a woman's uterus—the endometrium—grows outside the uterus. She also has lupus, which is a systemic autoimmune disease that occurs when your body's immune system attacks your own tissues and organs. And she has food allergies.

She has suffered her whole life from many of these illnesses.

And she has also been bullied because of them.

She can recall, as far back as high school, how people picked on her because she did not "look sick."

Even now, on her blog, that bullying continues. She often gets comments from blog readers about how she "doesn't look sick." They question whether she really has cerebral palsy. One of her followers even went so far as to write,

> You don't look like you have cerebral palsy, so are you doing this for attention?"

As you can imagine, this has been hard for Laura. Yet, she has not been deterred from blogging, writing about health, and sharing her passions with her followers.

And as a result, she is impacting the lives of others whom she meets because of her blog. She has met others in her own community with these same health issues, especially cerebral palsy. She has been able to connect with them, get to know them, and begin to build a community for people struggling with these issues.

For example, she was able to work with one family with a young daughter who had cerebral palsy. The family had been having a hard time navigating the healthcare system to get their daughter the care she needed. By meeting Laura through her blog, she was able to connect to them, meet them in-person, and begin to help them find the resources they needed.

In this way, she has been able to be an advocate those who do not have anyone to help them or do not have access to the right resources or the right people to whom to ask questions. Laura said that she feels that she has a role to play in being a voice for people who may not have a voice themselves.

For Laura, it is not just about recipes. It is not just about food. It is also not just about her own personal health experiences. It never was. Even when she first started her blog, she did so to build and maintain a community. And as her blog has grown and changed, so has that community. This lifetime of health issues, the bullying, and her experiences with blogging have opened up new motivations for maintaining her blog and talking about health—she sees it as being important to being able to help others around her.

Lisa's story

Lisa is another influencer I had the privilege of meeting during the course of my research. Lisa is multiracial and a lifestyle influencer. When we met, she was 35 years old.

Like Laura, Lisa suffers from severe chronic illnesses as well. When we met, she had just been diagnosed with Ehlers-Danlos syndrome, which is a family of genetic connective tissue disorders that causes brain lesions and fibromyalgia, among many other symptoms.[76]

In addition to her chronic illnesses, she has also suffered from other health issues such as infertility and postpartum depression. As well, her son has attention-deficit/hyperactivity disorder (ADHD), oppositional defiant disorder, and other sensory issues.

So Lisa has a lot to manage—not just her own health issues but also those of her son.

Yet, despite all of this, Lisa maintains a positive and hopeful outlook. Her experiences have made her incredibly passionate about writing about health—and her blog content is infused with this perspective. She uses her blog as a platform to talk about her illnesses, those of her son, and health topics more generally.

Morever, she calls herself, "very open" and "an open book" and tries to always write with a sense of honesty and transparency. She said her reason for doing this—putting herself out there like that—is driven by her desire to increase awareness of these issues among her followers. She wants to create a sense of understanding about her health issues—and health issues more generally—among them. By creating a dialogue about health, she feels that she is doing this.

Laura and Lisa both have substantial health issues. These limit their abilities to do things and cause them both a great deal of pain.

It would be completely understandable if these two women chose to view their health issues as barriers and to feel powerless and hopeless about them—a perspective that is often characterized as being fatalistic.

But they don't. In fact, Laura and Lisa see these in exactly the opposite way—they are motivators for them to engage in a conversation about health and try and change perceptions.

Why is this? How can they remain so positive in the face of such adversity?

Building on the last chapter's focus on influencers' perceptions of risk, it is interesting to see that while some influencers will not write about health because of all of the challenges certain health topics present, others will write about health inspite of them.

The rest of this chapter will hone in on what drives influencers to talk about health issues in spite of such barriers, with a particular focus on the concept of fatalism.

Understanding Fatalism and Its Role in Heath

Fatalism is defined as "a complex psychological cycle characterized by perceptions of hopelessness, worthlessness, meaninglessness, powerlessness, and social despair."[77]

As it relates to health, it is often the case that people who hold fatalistic beliefs about health may be at greater risk of health issues because they are less likely to engage in preventive behaviors.[78]

It has been theorized that certain ethnic groups such as Hispanic/Latinos and African Americans may be more likely to be fatalistic.[79,80] But, fatalism has also been associated with lower education and lower income. Thus, fatalism can be an influence on any number of people.

Social Norms and Fatalism

So, if fatalism can be found among many different types of people, then what accounts for it?

Social norms theory tells us that our individual behaviors are susceptible to environmental and interpersonal influences.[81] Essentially, what others around us do can often determine what we do.

It is widely believed that social norms can govern health-seeking and preventive behavior.[82] They do so by affecting individuals' perceived self-efficacy. We talked about perceived self-efficacy in Chapter 5 but to define it here for you again, it refers to the "beliefs that [people] can exert control over their motivation and behavior and over their social environment."[83] Thus, individuals' perceptions that they have the ability to make changes determines, at least in part, if they can, in fact, make and maintain those changes.

Fatalism, specifically, has been identified as one of the more powerful social norms that comes into play when it comes to perceived self-efficacy and behavior change. It can subjugate an individual's sense of self-efficacy in favor of perceptions of hopelessness and powerlessness. This, in turn, affects an individual's acceptability of preventive behaviors.

Or in simpler terms, fatalism is a concept that is formed within our social environment and our sense of fatalism influences whether we believe we have control over our health, and this perception influences whether we will take steps to better our health.

Thus fatalism is part of an individual's social and structural milieu, which impacts an individual's perceptions about whether they have the ability to address barriers and take steps to improve their own health and the health of others.

Influencers Are Not Fatalistic

So we understand now what fatalism is and its role in health. As well, we understand how fatalism is situated in the social contexts in which people live, work, and play.

It makes sense, then, to think that some online influencers would be fatalistic and others would not be. In short, it would make sense to think that the world of online influencers would parallel that of everyone else—that they would exist on a sort of "spectrum of fatalism," as the rest of society does.

However, findings from my research suggest that this is not the case. Results from the interviews I conducted suggest that few, if any, of them were fatalistic. As well, results from my survey of over 400 influencers from across the globe back this up.

That suggests that this population is not very fatalistic. Moreover, this also suggests that this population is special.

But why is that?

It Is Just the Great Unknown

Over the course of my research, most of the influencers did note that they thought their health was not solely in their control. Most seemed to think that there is an element of uncontrollability in health that all humans live with. They acknowledged that people cannot control everything and that sometimes things will happen that will not be related to how well an individual took care of himself or herself.

As Molly, a 38-year-old Caucasian sexual health influencer I met, said,

> [The likelihood of someone dying from a serious disease even if they get treatment for it] depends on the disease and other factors.

As well, Theresa, a 39-year-old African American mommy influencer I met, said,

> Better foods can encourage better health. But there are also genetics, so it's a combination.

Monique, the 39-year-old African American/Black fitness and health influencer, also said,

> You do your best, but I feel that if it's your time to go, it's your time to go. My mom used to smoke, got healthy, and she died anyway. Cancer in the liver. And it spread quickly. She was diagnosed in March and she died in June. I think the smoking contributed. But my dad smokes, has a pace maker, and is eighty-two and still kicking.

Finally, Amanda, the 34-year-old Caucasian parenting and lifestyle influencer, said,

> Without bringing in a religious voice, I think it's sometimes a product of our environment.

Despite this, almost all of them stated that there could be things that people can do to prevent illness or certain health conditions. Leah, a 29-year-old African American lifestyle influencer, said,

> Part of me believes [that] you need to put the extra effort forth ... part of me thinks it may not matter. I want to think [about] this a bit more. Your survey made me think about it.

As well, 35-year-old Lisa, from the beginning of the chapter, said,

> Genetics play a factor, but there are things you can do.

Amanda also said,

> I don't believe that our lives are predestined. We have control over the choices we make. If we smoke, it greatly increases the chance of cancer. So when that happens, that is a direct result of the choices they have made in their life.

And Theresa said,

> I don't agree with [the idea that if someone is meant to have a serious disease, it doesn't matter what doctors and nurses tell them to do, they will get the disease anyway]. We have to control what we can control, and you just don't know how things are going to turn out until you actually try.

Related to this, they noted that there were distinct things that could be done to change one's health. Consumption of healthier foods was named quite often. Theresa, the 39-year-old African American mommy influencer, said,

> Certain things we eat can contribute to issues, we can eat better foods and they can encourage better health.

Laura, the 34-year-old multiracial recipe influencer from the beginning of the chapter also said,

> Food matters sometimes. Diabetes runs in my family.

Finally, Amanda also said,

> The type of MS my mother had, we learned too late that if she had changed her diet, she may have been able to lead a bit healthier of a life. She still would have died, but it would have prolonged her life or made some things about her life a bit more manageable. I think there are times when we don't have control over what happens, like with my mother. I don't know that anything would have changed the outcome—it might have changed her life towards the end, made it easier, or given us another year."

As well, environmental changes such as handwashing, were also noted as possible preventative measures. Amanda said,

> There are lots of things in the environment that you can change that can help, like washing hands. Look at some other countries where certain diseases happen. These things can help curb diseases.

Ultimately, this group recognizes that little things can be done to encourage good health—and that while not everything is controllable, we should try to be healthier and not give up. As Amanda said,

> There are little things you can do to help change the outcome, instead of saying I am not going to do anything because I am going to get it anyway.

Thus, influencers are aware of the limits of an individual's ability to control their health, but also acknowledge that people can still do things to improve it.

So if we consider all of this together, influencers appear to be realistic, but not fatalistic. But why is this?

Well, generally speaking, influencers tend to be well educated and of higher socioeconomic status. And according to the literature, these things suggest that they would be less fatalistic. So you might be thinking that it has something to do with that.

But not all of the influencers who participated in my research could be characterized as being well educated and of higher socioeconomic income, and yet, they still exhibited non-fatalistic tendencies—perhaps even more so than those with more education and who had higher incomes.

So regardless of education, race/ethnicity, income level, geographic location, and other variables, it appears that influencers exhibit non-fatalistic tendencies.

But how can this be?

Well, I believe that influencers are a special ilk of people. Many of them started blogging to build some sort of network or community—even if it was just within their own family. I think this initial behavior of starting a blog exhibits their innate anti-fatalistic beliefs. I mean, I do not think they would have started their blog if they didn't think it would make a difference.

As well, I think many of them have continued to blog out of a desire to help themselves, their families, and others. We saw this with stories of Laura and Lisa as well as Sam and Monique.

Finally, I think because their content is always shared via personal narrative, they believe in sharing expertise through experience. In other words, a blog post that goes, "Today, my car broke down, and I did not think I could do anything about it so I sat in the car until someone happened to drive by and held me. The End," is, well, not much of a story. On the other hand, though, a post that shares a story about how someone's car broke down, so they put a message out in their favorite local Facebook group for help, and then someone came to help them, is such a better story—and one worth sharing. It is way more compelling. It draws you in and it connects you to the person.

Ultimately, their day-to-day lives become one long exercise in exerting their own will over the obstacles life throws at them. And their natural inclination for storytelling is what drives their desire to share those experiences with others. Their personal narrative approach to this storytelling conveys hope—and people connect to hope. It follows then, that hope is the foundation of their content. And hope is very anti-fatalistic.

Even Chronic Illness Does Not Appear to Produce Strong Conceptualizations of Fatalism

While all online influencers in my research appeared to be generally non-fatalistic, Laura's and Lisa's stories, which were shared at the beginning of this chapter, caught my attention because of how substantial their health issues were.

It would seem to me that if anyone would be fatalistic, it would be them. Yet, they were not. So their stories were of particular interest to me. I wanted to understand more about them and why they were the way they were.

You will recall that Laura is the 34-year-old multiracial recipe online influencer who suffers from spastic cerebral palsy, endometriosis, lupus, and food allergies, and Lisa is the 35-year-old multiracial lifestyle online influencer who suffers from Ehlers-Danlos. They are similar to one another in that they have very challenging health issues. They are also both college-educated and around the same age.

Yet, they also differ—Laura makes less than $50,000 annually, while Lisa makes over $100,000. As well, while they both happened to be multiracial, they differed in their individual racial/ethnic make-ups. Laura is African American and Native American, and Lisa is White and Asian.

Regardless of how these two influencers were similar or different, they shared similar views on the uncontrollable nature of health and referred to genetics as a key factor in this (which makes sense given the fact that the health issues they both suffer from are genetic ones).

They both talked about the advantages to trying to stay healthy despite such diseases. Laura talked about how staying healthy is most important exactly when there is the potential for a genetically inherited disease.

They were also both notably vocal about their perceptions of one's personal risk for health issues as well as one's ability to improve one's health through personal choice and action. They both maintained that consuming healthy foods specifically can contribute to overall improved health. Both of these influencers also perceived health as something worth striving for. They recognized that family history was important but that making healthy choices that can improve the severity of an inherited illness is still a worthy venture.

They both also shared how they knew people who suffered from illnesses but did not have strong support networks or did not know with whom to talk to get accurate information. This motivated them to feel a sense of responsibility to share their stories to increase understanding and awareness, and hopefully be a voice for those who did not have one.

It is unclear whether these two women are non-fatalistic because of their chronic illnesses or in spite of them, but it does suggest that there is something unique about them and their shared experiences with health that may inform or reinforce this worldview. Despite being burdened by health issues and prior evidence that would suggest that they would be highly fatalistic, they are not. Moreover, despite prior research that suggests that fatalism may be a function of demographics such as race/ethnicity, income, and/or education, the experiences of these two online influencers suggests otherwise.

Previously, I noted why I think influencers are not fatalistic, generally speaking. In the case of these two women, I find their non-fatalistic attitudes to be remarkable. I have to believe that while influencers are not fatalistic generally, Laura's and Lisa's illnesses only serve to intensify these perspectives. These women see their illnesses as opportunities to educate and to build awareness—all in the hopes of helping themselves and others—in order that this dialogue and increased awareness may someday lead to better therapies, treatments, and possibly more permanent solutions and cures.

There is arguably a lot for them to fall back on—and blame—if they did not want to talk about health or try and make a difference. Their health issues are chronic—not something that can easily be fixed with one pill or a diet change.

In response, they could be mad. Or sad. They could be private about their illnesses. They could still blog but refuse to make health a focus. But they are not. They do not. They keep pushing. Motivated by something that is really personal and intangible. Fatalism is just NOT a characteristic of who they are.

Final Reflections

So influencers appear to not be fatalistic. That opens up a lot of possibilities for health communicators because it seems that regardless of the fact that there may be risk in talking about an issue they are still motivated to write and talk about health topics to try and help themselves and others.

This is also why it is so important for you to get to know your influencers. You should know them and their interests and their passions. But you should also get to know their personal health stories. Both those that they suffer from as well as those that may affect their family, friends, and community.

Understanding where they are in their life and how health is affecting them will be key to engaging them successfully.

It is helpful to know if they are suffering and cannot really participate in something. It is also helpful to understand if there are new topics or issues that they can work with you on. This helps position your work and helps show how health is relevant to them and their lives.

Thus far in the book, we have talked about why influencers are influential, the relationships they build and maintain, and the business of influencers. We have taken a peak at their perceptions of health issues, including barriers and what motivates them. We know they are not fatalistic so as marketers, there is an opportunity to get our messages distributed. But how do you talk with them and what kinds of messages do they want to share. This is the focus of the next chapter.

Chapter 7

The Importance of the Message

mes·sage | /ˈmesij/ | noun
A communication in writing, in speech, or by signals.

A few years ago, I was part of a team, which was developing messages and materials to support the release of a new type of flu vaccine that was coming to market. Prior flu vaccines had protected against three different flu viruses, and this new one was designed to protect against four (two type A flu viruses and two type B flu viruses).[84]

Our team's goal was to clearly and succinctly communicate that this new vaccine was coming out, what it meant that it covered four viruses instead of three, and provide people with information about what to do to learn more and get vaccinated.

To help consumers understand this new vaccine and how it differed from prior vaccines, we developed some new communication materials that aimed to explain these things.

Or at least we thought we did.

Before approving the materials that had been created, we needed to test them with audiences. So we focus group tested them with a mix of consumers to see what they thought.

During this process, group participants were shown the materials and asked for their thoughts about them. And they did not like them. But not only was their feedback to the materials not good, it was actually really negative. These negative reactions clearly meant that they did not like the materials. But the strength of the reactions suggested to us that something else was really wrong with them.

We were stumped though. Clearly the materials did not work, but what could possibly cause *such* a negative backlash?

The focus group moderator dug in further with the group, trying to ask more questions to tease out what really was going on; and after some additional probing, we got it. The materials had been written using really scientific language so the participants were not easily able to understand them. And when we asked them to share their thoughts about the materials, they could only respond with frustration.

While getting such negative feedback to materials is never easy for communicators to hear, it actually is a really important part of the message and materials development process because it helps ensure that the messages being created will be received well by the audience for whom they are intended.

And for us, this feedback was invaluable. It helped us understand that we had gotten it wrong with the versions we tested. The feedback made us go back to the materials and reassess how we were communicating the messages. Without the input from these consumers, we would have put out materials that ultimately would not have been useful to anyone.

A few years later, I was conducting some other research related to HPV vaccination. During the course of this study, I asked a number of influencers to participate in some interviews about writing about HPV vaccination. During the course of these interviews, I asked them about whether or not they would be willing to write about HPV vaccination on their blogs or in social media.

And the responses were pretty unanimous. The participants all said that, yes, they would write about the HPV vaccine.

Driving this willingness to write about the vaccine was its particular connection to cervical cancer prevention, which they felt was really important information their followers should know about. As well, they thought that the information was important to share with their followers who had children who may be approaching "critical [health] milestones" such as the age when children can get the HPV vaccine.

I know. We have spent A LOT of time in this book talking about how vaccination is one of those topics that many influencers do not like to write about because of the controversy. So this may seem contradictory. You might read that last paragraph and think, "But wait, you've been saying all along that most influencers do not often like to write about vaccination." Or perhaps, you read that last paragraph and thought, "Great! So in fact, influencers WILL write about vaccinations!"

Either way, it is not that simple.

As we have previously been discussing, influencers may choose to write about controversial topics – but often, and especially when the topic is controversial, they will want to write about it their own way. In a way that makes them feel comfortable with writing about the topic. And in a way that they think their followers will respond to so that it will not invite too much, if any, negative backlash.

In the case of the HPV vaccination story, this same principle held true. The influencers said that their willingness to write about this topic was conditional on their ability to present the information in a manner they thought most appropriate for their followers. For most of the influencers, this meant presenting the topic in a factual manner, not one imbued with emotion. And not one that would invite debate. As well, they thought that highlighting the fact that the content was up-to-date, accurate, and from a reliable source would help it be received as "good for [their] readers and their [readers'] children."

Another thought the influencers had on how to frame the messages included tailoring the message to an influencer's specific followership. For one influencer, who wrote for parents with special needs children, this meant providing a rationale for getting the vaccination that would be in line with the values of those parents and their children's health needs. They all also said that they would highlight the "protection" and "safety" aspects of getting the vaccine because those would be the most important aspects to share with their followers.

Moreover, all the influencers said that critical to framing any post on HPV vaccination is focusing on giving parents all the information so that they can make informed decisions. One participant specifically suggested providing the following types of messages:

> What [the vaccine] is, why kids need it, and a serious discussion on the risks. Perhaps a paragraph on making an informed decision yourself. I think knowledge is power—no matter what your final personal decision is.

Just as we heard from Sam in Chapter 4, these influencers are willing to share information because they want to give their followers all the right information on a topic so that they can make the best decision for themselves and their family. But they will not go so far as to recommend it, especially when it comes to a topic that is somewhat controversial. They want to leave the final decision up to their followers to make.

These two stories exemplify how messaging is critical to conveying important health topics accurately and in ways that consumers can comprehend. The first demonstrates how messaging influences consumer comprehension, while the second provides insight into the strategies that influencers use to message challenging topics.

Unfortunately, complex messaging is often the root of the problem. We talk too much. We take too long to get the point. We explain things in ways that require people to spend too much time figuring out what our point is. And because health can be complex and multi-faceted, this is too often an occurrence in health communication.

Moreover, in 2015, Microsoft conducted a study that found that people's attention spans were generally decreasing. Through their study, they found that people now generally lose concentration after 8 s. The average attention span for the notoriously inattentive goldfish is nine seconds.[85] So, yes, we, as humans, now have shorter attention spans than goldfish.

We are now living in a world where it is harder and harder to get people's attention, keep their attention, and convey complex information in a way that the average consumer can understand. The ability to communicate simply while still ensuring the totality of the message is a valuable—but difficult—skill. Yet, if we are going to successfully disseminate health information well into the future, this is a skill we have to hone. Because of this, messaging—and the importance of how you craft the message—is worth some discussion. This is the focus of this chapter.

Online Influencer Preferences for Health Messages

We have talked a lot throughout this book about how online influencers are persuasive and how they can help support health initiatives. However, health is a complex subject and messaging health topics can be tricky. Therefore, understanding online influencers' preferences for health messages and what they consider important (or not important) is essential for communicators seeking to work with them.

During the course of my research, I wanted to better understand how online influencers perceived certain types of health messages, so I chose a couple of different ones and asked them for their feedback.

I was conducting my research toward the end of the Zika virus outbreak in 2017, so I decided to test two different types of Zika-related messages (a risk message and a prevention message) that had been created by CDC and were publically available at the time. One communicated the risk of contracting Zika by portraying the transmission cycle for the virus (from mosquito to human and back to mosquito and from human to human). It used an infographic-type design to do this. This represented the risk message in my study. See Figure 7.1.

The other communicated how to protect oneself in order to prevent getting infected with Zika. It provided a practical guide for how to prevent Zika and included a list of product types that can help consumers protect themselves. This represented the prevention message in my study. See Figure 7.2.

I also tested the combination of the two messages together as a third message option. This acted as a risk & prevention combined message type.

After surveying over 400 influencers globally, I took their responses about which message type they preferred and

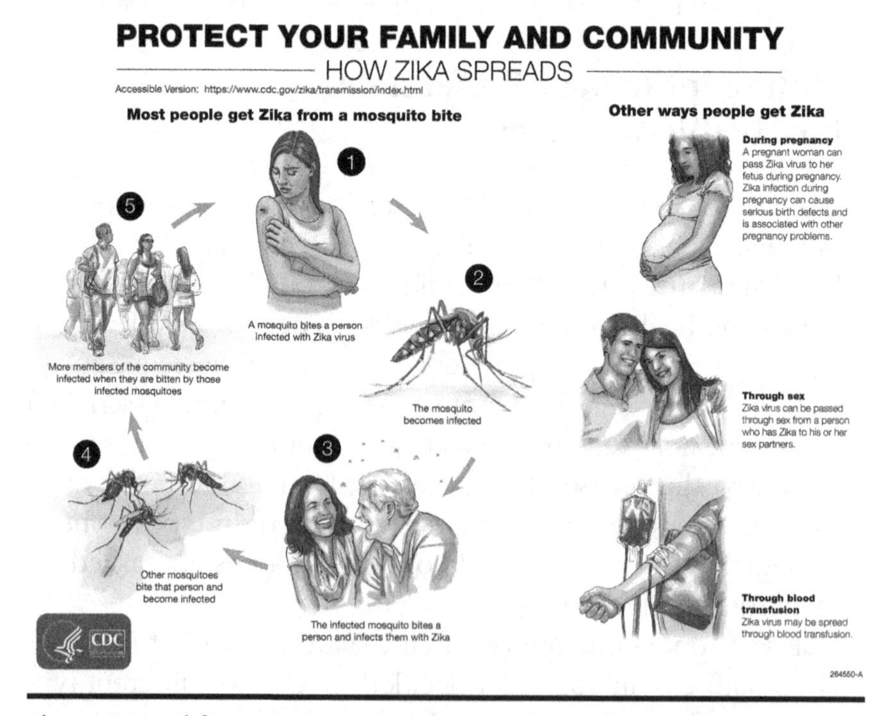

Figure 7.1 Risk message (www.cdc.gov/zika/comm-resources/infographics.html).

The products below can help protect you from Zika.
Use these items to build your own Zika prevention kit.

Bed Net

- Keep mosquitoes out of your room day and night. If your room is not well screened, use this bed net when sleeping or resting.
- Mosquitoes can live indoors and will bite at any time, day or night.

Insect Repellent

- Insect repellent will help keep mosquitoes from biting you.
- Use only an EPA-registered insect repellent.
- Always follow the directions on the bottle.
- Do not spray repellent on the skin under clothing.
- If you are also using sunscreen, apply sunscreen first and insect repellent second.
- When used as directed, these insect repellents are proven safe and effective even for pregnant and breastfeeding women.

Condoms

- During sex, it is possible to get Zika virus from a partner who has Zika. If you have sex during your pregnancy, you should use condoms the right way every time.
- Not having sex eliminates the risk of getting Zika through sex.

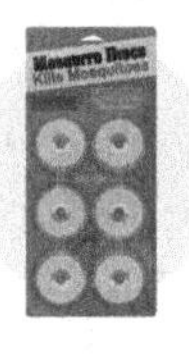

Standing Water Treatment Tabs

- Use water treatment tabs to kill larvae in standing water around your house. Do not put them in water you drink.
- Always follow directions on the package.
- When used as directed, these tabs will not harm you or your pets (dogs and cats).

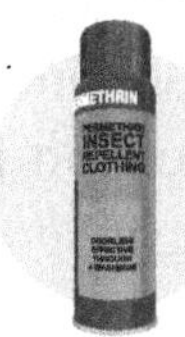

Permethrin Spray

- Spray your clothing and gear with permethrin to help protect you from mosquito bites.
- Always follow the directions on the bottle. Reapply as directed.
- Do not spray permethrin on your skin.

www.cdc.gov/zika

CS289371- March 1, 2018

Figure 7.2 Prevention message (www.cdc.gov/zika/pdfs/zika-kit-flyer.pdf).

why (which was an open-ended question where influencers could write in their responses) and analyzed the themes that emerged from that feedback. And the findings from this analysis did reveal something about what they value in messaging and content.

Overall, the prevention message (Figure 7.2) was preferred the most. Common reasons that the influencers gave for why they selected the prevention message included that it was "more informative," had "better organization and graphics," and had "better info and [was] more practical."

One influencer wrote,

> It's easier to understand the way the material is presented.

Another wrote,

> It is solution oriented rather than telling the history of mosquitoes and how they bite people.

Ultimately, the online influencers who preferred the prevention message appeared to do so because of the practicality and utility of the message, which signifies how important it is to them to give their followers information that is actionable and useful.

After the prevention message, the risk message (Figure 7.1) was the second most preferred message. The most common reason influencers gave for preferring this message was because it was "reader- and user-friendly." A less frequently cited reason for preferring this message was because it provided "solutions." As one online influencer wrote,

> It may not show you how to protect yourself, but it gives you information on how it is spread.

Thus, the use of visuals drove influencer preference for this message. This message type's use of visuals to tell the Zika transmission story suggests that imagery helps increase comprehension of a more complex health message such as one about the transmission of a virus. This also provides insight into …why influencers prefer visual formats for messaging—especially when the topic is about a complex health issue. That is, visuals help their followers understand the messages more easily and therefore make them more receptive to them.

However, the fact that providing actionable or solution-oriented content was cited less frequently by the influencers as a reason for preferring the risk message means that most of them did not think it did. This suggests, then, that the lack of actionable information in the risk message was noticed by the majority of influencers and may have been why influencers preferred the prevention message more than the risk message.

These findings suggest that while visuals are nice, and often preferred by influencers, they still only serve to more easily convey whatever the core message is; and if that message is not complete, the visual depiction of that message will also not be complete. In this case, the risk message only told part of the story, e.g., how Zika is transmitted and not how to prevent getting it. This omission was not lost on the influencers.

Finally, the third message option—the combination of the risk and prevention message types—was the one type that online influencers preferred the least. Those who preferred to share the two messages together said they would do so because the two messages provided "better info and [were] more practical" and that they were "more actionable," "more informative," and they provided "solutions." For example, one online influencer said,

> One shows the cause and the other gives prevention measures.

Another said,

> The first one tells me about how to prevent being infected by Zika, and the second one sheds light on how Zika spreads. Both are relevant.

Finally, a third said,

> I would share both of the materials with my readers just to err on the side of caution. It helps raise awareness for how the Zika virus spreads, as well as how to take preventative measures against it—pregnant or not.

This suggests that when these two message types are used together, they provide more information and more solutions for people.

However, the combination of the two message types also seemed to cause some confusion for influencers. Only a few comments from online influencers who chose this message type included qualities such as being "easier to follow" and "easier to read." This suggests that using two separate messages together to provide both the risk and the prevention sides of a health issue can still result in complicating the message.

If you consider this feedback collectively, it is apparent that clear and actionable messaging is often preferred. Influencers like to be able to tell their followers what they can do to prevent or treat an issue. Lists are a great way to do this because they help make the message feel organized and simple and they make things easy and memorable. The prevention message type did just that.

As well, visual appeal is very compelling with influencers because they help make complex information comprehendible. This was the case with the risk message type. Preference for the risk message type had to do with what influencers thought their readers would like and be able to easily understand—and the message type's use of visuals was a primary factor in this preference.

Finally, the fact that the option to use the two messages together was liked the least buttresses this overarching preference and need for clear and simple messaging. While we often want to give people all the information about a topic, sometimes providing too much information can be overwhelming to people, causing them to be overall less receptive to it.

Ultimately, it is important to understand what online influencers want in terms of health messages, what they think their followers will enjoy, and how much information is too much. Working with influencers to create messages that will stand out, resonate with followers, *and* convey important health messages accurately is hard to do. But done right, it can be really successful. Below are some tips you can use to achieve these aims.

Tips for Communicators

As we have seen, messaging is important when working with influencers. As you begin to work with them, you may want to keep the following messaging best practices in mind to ensure the successful dissemination of your messages by influencers to their followers.

Remember the Importance of the Messaging Document

We talked about this in Chapter 5, but it is important to reiterate here. When working with influencers, always have your messages organized and prioritized into an easy-to-understand messaging document. You will recall that your messaging document lays out all the important points that you want your influencers to convey. It provides important links and graphics, as well as draft or example social media posts that the influencers can easily copy and paste on to their blog or in social media. The messaging document is also important because it helps ensure that the most important messages are captured and highlighted for influencers making it easy for them to post the right message.

When putting together your messaging document, think about the audience you are trying to reach. Is it a scientific audience or a lay audience? Is this an existing health issue that people are already familiar with or is it a new one that you will need to introduce to your audience? Your answers to these questions will help you successfully craft your messaging document in a way that achieves your goals.

Write Simply

One of the myths about writing simply is that you have to "dumb down" your content so that everyone can read it.[86] But that is not exactly true. Rather than "dumbing your content down," you should write for your audience. Use the language your audience understands and feels comfortable with. You would not want to write in very scientific terms for a lay audience, but you also would not want to eliminate all complexity if your audience is composed of medical professionals.

Choose Your Words Carefully

Be thoughtful about which words you are using including jargon, technical terms, and abbreviations, which may make it harder for people to comprehend what it is you are trying to say.[87]

Organization Is Key[88]

Be clear about what the aim of your initiative is. Make sure you prioritize the messages that are most important so that the influencers know what to focus on first. Secondary messages are nice, but they may not make it into a post, so make sure to highlight what you really want disseminated—and be okay with the fact that those secondary messages may not get shared.

Remember Your Disclosure Statements

We talked at length about disclosures in Chapter 3, but as it relates to messaging and influencers, it bears repeating. Disclosure language is REALLY important and is one of the required things that should be included in the messaging document. Moreover, trustworthy influencers and the networks they belong to will *want* to have this language from you. They will ask you for it if you have left it out of the messaging document. That is how you know who the good ones really are.

Finally, while we have also talked about this earlier, it is relevant and important to mention here again as we close out our discussion of messaging—you have to trust your influencers with your message. It is one of the scariest things for marketers and communicators about working with online influencers, but it is true—you need to trust your influencers to follow your guidance and write solid and on-message posts in their own voices and in a way that is appropriate for their followers.

Final Reflections

Working with influencers is not complicated, but it does require nuance when building relationships with them and crafting messaging that speaks to their interests and their followers' needs. Just as we saw in the HPV vaccine story that we started this chapter with, working with influencers to develop approaches for messaging challenging health topics can help you figure out the best way to get your message out to your intended target audiences. So listen to them and get their thoughts.

Moreover, by trusting your influencers with your message and working with them as partners, you can help ensure that the health topic is messaged accurately and that it will be positively received by consumers. Keeping these things in mind as you work on developing messaging will help you deliver quality content to your target audiences, via influencers, successfully.

Often though, influencers want easy-to-understand and shareable creative to accompany the messaging. And with the rise of visual platforms such as Instagram, good creative is increasingly important in social media, especially for influencers. Understanding the importance of great—not just good—creative will be the focus of the next chapter.

Chapter 8

The Importance of Great—Not Good—Creative

cre·a·tive | \ krē-ˈā-tiv \ | adjective
Relating to or involving the imagination or original ideas, especially in the production of an artistic work.

In 2018, I was working on a initiative with a large public health agency to promote preconception health and healthy pregnancy. Healthy pregnancy is not a new topic—it has been talked about often in different ways and on different platforms by all sorts of different people, campaigns, and organizations. Moreover, as we were planning this initiative, we did not have any new information or data about healthy pregnancy to share that would help us overcome this challenge of issue fatigue and help capture people's attention. We needed to find a new way to discuss the topic that would provide a fresh perspective and get people talking.

Up until that point, most initiatives that promoted preconception health had focused on women's health and the role of the woman in having a healthy pregnancy. Few communication initiatives had paid attention to and focused their message on the role of fathers in having a health pregnancy. So we decided that quotes would be our creative approach.

With our creative concept now confirmed, we identified and reached out to a few online influencers asking them to write about the topic. One of the major influencers I reached out to—and who agreed to write about it—was Pregnant Chicken.

In our work with Pregnant Chicken for this initaitive, we followed all the best practices we have been discussing throughout this book. We prepared our messaging document with our key talking points, links, and images. We brainstormed and collaborated together about ideas for content approaches.

But in the end, we let her decide how to frame the message for her followers. We trusted her to know what would work best—and what we got was truly amazing and inspired.

It was also *totally* non-traditional for a public health campaign.

Her post, which featured an image of a circle of men in white sperm-looking suits and an animated GIF of a dancing penis, was both edgy and humorous. Its use of these kinds of visuals helped her catch her followers' attention and draw them in so that they would go on and read the actual health information. You can see snapshots from her post below.

Pregnant Chicken's Post on the Father's Role in a Health Pregnancy[a]

Sperm Health and 10 Things That Can Affect Fertility

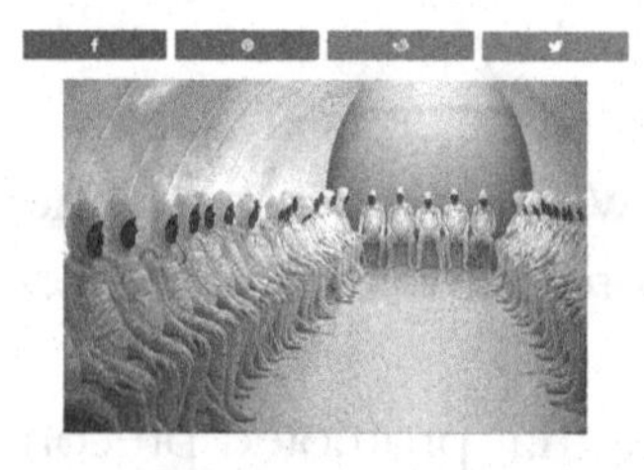

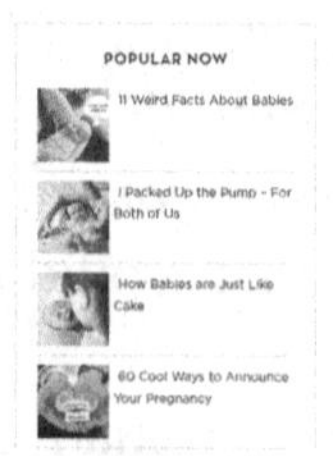

[a] https://pregnantchicken.com/sperm-health.

This use of humor and edginess to talk about everyday issues, and even more serious topics, is an approach we also saw used by Dooce.com blogger, Heather Armstrong, in Chapter 2. As we discussed, Armstrong's famous sense of humor and honest and transparent writing about her personal life has garnered her millions of loyal followers over the years. They adore her content, following it regularly, and they keep coming back for more.

This same use of humor and stimulating content is one way that health messages can be conveyed.

But of course, while humor and "edginess" can attract attention, the message still needs to be accurate. And, in fact, Pregnant Chicken blog post was right on-message according to our messaging document.

So she did both—talked accurately about a health issue but used humor and edginess to make the issue relatable and attract attention to the post.

And her approach worked! Pregnant Chicken's post generated more than 8,000 page views and had a reach on Facebook of more than 40,000. Thus, clearly, she was able to engage her blog readers and social media in a dialogue about preconception health. She was able to do this because she talked about an well-known health issue in a new way, but also one that her followers could relate to. She drew people in with humor and was able to keep them there to read the main message.

Her approach also stayed true to her brand, which resonated with followers because they did not see the post as being at odds with everything else that she writes. And because of all of this, the preconception health message got out there to many people who may not have otherwise seen it.

In Chapter 7, we discussed the importance of messaging and we touch briefly on visuals as well. Great creative and visualizations often work alongside good messaging and are another great way to convey complex information in an easy-to-view and -understand format. This will be the focus of this chapter.

The Importance of Visuals

Have you ever checked your Facebook feed around dinner time only to see a plethora of food-related posts—either from friends checking into restaurants, or Instagramming their meal, or from recipe bloggers you follow—and gotten hungry? Or ordered food? Or decided what to cook for dinner that night?

Well, if this sounds familiar, then you have actually exhibited a very specific consumer behavior called "visual decision-making."[89] This phenomenon affects what people do, where they go, and what they buy all based on the visuals they see.

And it is not all food related. For instance, there is a whole industry built on using photos to entice travel purchases. Destination Marketing Organizations, or DMOs, for short, are disrupting the travel industry by using "visual influencers" to photograph beautiful and exotic destinations in the hopes of captivating and attracting more travelers to them.[90]

For companies and brands, this trend in using visuals to communicate the benefits of a product or service opens up a world of opportunity to attract, engage, and inspire more people to take action and make purchases.

Visuals are impactful in other ways as well. For instance, the use of color in visuals is proven to increase people's willingness to read a piece of content by 80 percent. As well, retention of heard information is said to increase from 10 to 65 percent when paired with a visual.

And of course, in our digital world, We are all familiar with just how important and immensely popular visuals are. But just in case you do not know what I am talking about, let me share a few statistics with you to set the stage:

- More than half (54 percent) of Internet users have posted original photos/videos to websites.[91]
- Nearly half (47 percent) of Internet users share photos/ videos they find elsewhere online.

- People who shop on their phones say images are the most important feature when making a purchase decision,[92] and it is estimated that more than 40 percent of consumers are influenced to purchase something by the photos they see specifically on Instagram.

So there you have it. Visuals are key. They are powerful. They are emotive. They are vital conduits of information. And they also act as important stimuli for behavior change.

But there are so many types of visuals. In just the last few paragraphs, we have already mentioned a number of types—video, photos, and graphics. So how do you know what to use and which one is better than the others in driving consumers to engage and take action?

Well, let's dig into the various types of visuals, shall we? We'll start with video.

The Rise—and Dominance—of Video. Video is not new. For more than 15 years, Internet users have been sharing video content.[93] And consumers' appetites for video is voracious. It is projected that this year (2019), people will spend approximately the same amount of time online as they do watching television (3 hours per day).[94] In fact, 45 whole minutes of an average person's Internet time will be spent watching video *just* on mobile devices. Because of all of this video consumption, it is also predicted that companies will spend less money on television ads and more money on Web video this year.

So yes, people love video. Moreover, they love watching videos across all different types of platforms, e.g., YouTube, Instagram, Facebook, and Snapchat.

They also love watching all forms of video—from short- to long-form content and everything in between. Below I describe three of the most popular platforms for video—YouTube, Instagram, and Facebook.

YouTube

YouTube, which differs from other social media platforms in that it only supports video content, remains a major platform for video to this day.[95] YouTube reports that as of 2018, it now has over 1.8 billion users every month—and that is just the people who are logged in.[96] That means that YouTube has more users than Google's Gmail service, making the platform Google's most popular service. This also means YouTube is nearing Facebook, which is the world's largest platform with 2 billion+ monthly users.

Much of the content that has been created on YouTube is content from influencers—both layperson and celebrity. In fact, YouTube influencers have become so popular, that many of them are known as "YouTube Stars." For example, Felix "PewDiePie" Kjellberg is a Swedish YouTuber who is one of the most popular YouTube Stars worldwide, with over 62 million subscribers. His content consists mainly of Let's Play commentaries (which are instructional videos for playing video games) and comedy.

In addition to this kind of short-form content, YouTube also features long-form content. For instance, YouTube offers scripted content by stars such as Kevin Hart and Demi Lovato.

A final content type that is visual and engaging to users is the YouTube slider. The YouTube slider pulls video content from YouTube (and other video sites) and turns them into a carousel of videos that can live on a website or blog.[97] This tool allows online influencers to easily pull your content into existing sliders they are already using on their blog or website. Because of this, it helps embed your message into their existing messaging and connect it with other similar content. This helps with the visibility of your video as users may stumble upon it while viewing other related content. It, therefore, allows your message to reach viewers who might not otherwise see it.

Instagram

In addition to images, Instagram also supports basic video content. Additionally, it offers stories, which is immensely popular with a reported 200 million users every month. Stories allow users to post photos and videos that vanish after 24 hours.[98] Like YouTube, much of the content created using the Stories feature is from influencers—both layperson and celebrity.

Stories appear in a bar at the top of user Instagram feeds, and when a user has posted a new story, a ring appears around the user's profile photo. To view a user's story, tap on his/her profile photo, and all of the content posted in the last 24 hours will appear in the full screen of your mobile device. This content will play in chronological order from oldest to newest. Unlike regular posts, there are no likes or public comments on Stories.

Finally, Instagram also offers IGTV, which offers longer form video content. IGTV launched in 2018 and allows videos up to 10 minutes in length or, if a user is verified or popular on Instagram, videos up to 60 minutes in length. IGTV, however, has found limited success so far.[99] The slow growth of IGTV has been attributed to how it was launched. At its inception, IGTV engaged YouTube Stars to help support its launch, thinking that they would bring their YouTube audiences over to IGTV. However, that has not been the case. As Scott Fisher, founder of Select Management Group, which is the digital talent company that represents online influencers, said

> [That while some die-hard fans are watching, the audience for IGTV] isn't fully there yet … even huge celebrities and influencers are struggling to get the same types of views [on IGTV] they get on YouTube or their feed.

Facebook

Finally, like Instagram, Facebook also supports basic video content. However, in 2016, the social media giant launched Facebook Live. Live is Facebook's answer to live video streaming.[100] You can easily start broadcasting live to your friends and followers via your mobile device by tapping the live stream icon on the Facebook app. Once you are done broadcasting, it will post as a video to your feed. It is recommended that the minimum amount of time you should go live for is at least 10 minutes, and you can stay live for up to 4 hours.[101] Again, similar to YouTube and Instagram, Live is often used by both layperson and celebrity influencers. However, it is also popular for news and other live coverage events. Since 2016, when Live launched, there have been more than 3.5 billion Live broadcasts.[102]

A final note on video is that while the aforementioned platforms are very popular with billions of users globally, not all generations of people are using the same social media. Generation Z-ers, who are those born somewhere between the mid-1990s and mid-2000s, have grown up with social media and they view it entirely differently from those of us who did not. As a result, social media is a part of their daily content diet. They regularly use new and emerging social media technologies and are not necessarily loyal to one platform over another.

Specifically, video is a regular part of the way they communicate and connect with others online. And many of the new applications and platforms they participate on are driven by video. An example that is currently very popular with this group is a mobile application called Houseparty, which utilizes group video chats. Think about it as a way to have a house party—only everyone is on their mobile devices video chatting virtually. Totally wild, I know.

GIFs and Memes. Other forms of popular visual content that are easily shared via social media include GIFs and memes. Both of these refer to those popular images you might have seen shared online that usually include an image which is accompanied by white or black block text that has been overlaid on it. They can be animated or static and there is usually some sort of a humorous or ironic association between the image and the text, which is what makes them eye-catching and funny.

The format and content of GIFs and memes help catch people's attention while disseminating messages using humor and irony. This is what makes them funny, engaging, and worth sharing with others.

It is important to note that while memes, specifically, have become popularized with the advent of social media, in fact, they pre-date social media. Richard Dawkins, who is considered to be the father of memes, defined memes in 1976 as

> Any idea, behavior or trend that has the ability to transmit from person to person.[103]

So memes did not always refer to visual content, but rather, they were ideas that were shared from person to person. Today's memes build on this idea by transmitting messages and information visually and virtually from person to person.

In fact, today's memes have become so well-known and popular online that they are now considered,

> A part of the 'web diet' of many Internet users, casually popping up in visits to platforms such as YouTube, Facebook, and Reddit.[104]

And there are more than 12,000 of them online.[105] Similar to GIFs in look and feel, the popularity of memes makes them unique because they have achieved a certain level of online cultural significance. Popular memes from across the Internet include the late Grumpy Cat, Sad Keanu, and Is Ryan Gosling Cuter than a Puppy?. Examples of these are below.

Grumpy Cat[a] *Sad Keanu*[b] *Is Ryan Gosling Cuter than a Puppy?*[c]

[a] https://sayingimages.com/grumpy-cat-memes/.
[b] https://imgflip.com/memegenerator/Sad-Keanu.
[c] www.her.ie/life/gallery-is-ryan-gosling-cuter-than-a-puppy-32305.

In fact, memes can reach such a high level of visibility and popularity that they take over more mainstream media conversations and may even crash websites and dominate consumers' online search behaviors. This phenomenon has become known as "Breaking the Internet," which *TIME Magazine* defined as,

> Engineering one story to dominate Facebook and Twitter at the expense of more newsworthy things.

One popular meme that you may be familiar with that has "broken the Internet" is "Alex from Target." "Alex from Target" became a social media sensation in just 1 day after a photo of him working at Target was taken and went viral.[106] It became so popular that within a couple days after the photo went viral, he was scheduled to appear on "The Ellen DeGeneres Show."

Alex from Target[a]

[a] www.j-14.com/posts/alex-from-target-now-137935/.

Moreover, in response to this viral photo, other various Internet memes ensued. These mimicked the photo by sharing photos of other teenagers in jobs, e.g., Kieran from T-Mobile and Steve from Starbucks. And Alex impersonators started showing up posting videos on the video service, Vine. Alex's Twitter followers went from 144 to more than 600,000.

And the photo, indeed, broke the Internet because, just as TIME Magazine defined it, the popularity of the photo was at the expense of other issues that were arguably more important at the time. As Sree Sreenivasan, Chief Digital Officer at the Metropolitan Museum of Art, said,

> This just shows you it is another Tuesday on the Internet... There is all these important things going on like the election, but some portion of the Internet is paying attention to something else.

So who was "Alex from Target" and how did he become an Internet sensation?

Well, "Alex" is Alex Lee, a 16-year-old from Texas. But while we know his identity, it is still a bit murky how this photo came to be.

It would make sense to think that Target would have been behind this sensation, but despite the attention the photo received, Target denied being a part of this, stating,

> Let us be completely clear, we had absolutely nothing to do with the creation, listing or distribution of the photo.

One story that emerged about who was behind the viral photo was that the marketing start-up, Breakr, intentionally created it by leaking the photo and creating the hashtag #alexfromtarget. They said,

> We wanted to see how powerful the fan girl demographic was by taking an unknown good-looking kid and Target employee from Texas to overnight viral Internet sensation.

However, this story has also been disputed.

So we may never really know who started the phenomenon that became "Alex from Target," but regardless of how this sensation started, it took off, capturing the attention of millions of people all across the Internet and beyond.

For health communicators, it is hard to compete with the viral popularity of such GIFs, memes, and other content that "breaks the Internet."

We compare our messages with those that "go viral" and wonder "how can we do that?"

But, just as the TIME Magazine definition stated, these things are engineered. They don't happen organically. Things rarely just go viral. Most often, the high level of visibility of this kind of content is driven by ad dollars and other related promotional efforts.

For health, it is important to keep this in mind because we are often not working with the same level of budget or celebrity that can drive similar levels of content sharing, website clicks, and Google searches. We need to keep a bit of perspective when comparing our initiatives with those other larger and more well-known and well-funded campaigns.

It is also worth mentioning that while the funny and ironic format of GIFs and memes can make something very shareable—and that is ideally what we want for health messages—using this format for health messages should be done with careful consideration.

Taking serious subjects and using them in this format if not done appropriately can be disrespectful to people effected by the issue in real life, or it can be perceived as making light of an issue that is serious. Both of these can invite negative feedback from social media users and ultimately have the opposite effect of what you want.

Some good examples of how to use this medium to promote your health messages are below.

In the first example, the popular Ryan Gosling Hey Girl meme is used to promote a message about handwashing. It states,

Handwashing[a]	*Cold and Flu Prevention*[b]	*Vaccination*[c]
	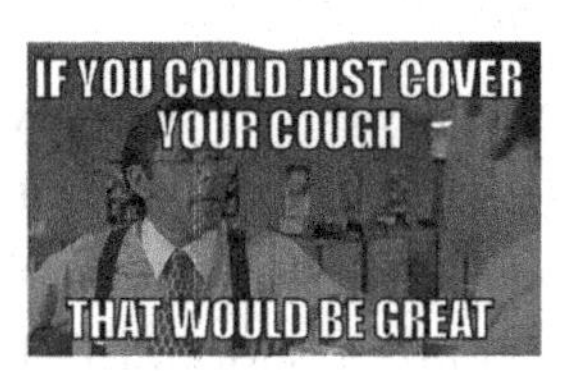	

[a] www.getreadyforflu.org/EcardGoslingGerms.htm.
[b] https://me.me/i/if-you-could-go-ahead-and-cover-your-f-cking-8815073.
[c] https://thelogicofscience.com/2015/10/12/100-bad-arguments-against-vaccines/.

> Hey Girl, did you wash your hand before dinner tonight? Cool. Because you know, germs.

The second meme features an image from the cult movie, Office Space, and uses this to promote cold and flu prevention. It states,

> If you could just cover your cough that would be great.

Finally, the third uses the famous fist pump baby meme to promote vaccination, stating,

> I was fully vaccination along with millions of people and guess who's perfectly fine? Me and millions of people.

These memes take popular culture phenomena and tie health messages to them. They are shareable because people recognize the image, but they also do a good job of choosing the right words for the message and tying those words to the right image so as not to create something that may be offensive or make to light of a more serious health issue.

Data Visualization. A final visual content area that is worth some brief discussion is data visualization. Data visualization is another form of visual content that describes "any effort to help people understand the significance of data by placing it in a visual context."[107]

Data visualization is valuable when you are talking about understanding large data sets more easily or taking concepts that are complex and being able to explain more easily through the use of visuals. Visualizing these data makes it easier for the human brain to process the information.[108] That is why so many reports now include tables, graphs, and infographics, which visually distill the main points and make it easier to understand.

We saw how data visualization can help simplify complex concepts in Chapter 7 when we discussed the Zika virus infographic that I tested. CDC's use of this kind of data visualization to explain Zika virus transmission helped make the concept simpler and easier to understand for consumers.

Ultimately, there are many different types of creative that work well online and that can be developed for use with online influencers. But what kinds of visuals do they want? To understand this a little better, let's review some of their feedback specifically on the creative elements of the Zika messages that I tested and that we started discussing in Chapter 7.

Online Influencer Preference for Creative

As discussed in Chapter 7, in my research, I wanted to explore online influencers' perceptions of different types of health messages, and to do so, I shared three different types of messages (the first communicating the risk of contracting Zika, the second communicating how to prevent getting infected with Zika, and the third combining the risk and prevention messages). See Figures 7.1 and 7.2 for these messages.

You will recall that the prevention message was the most preferred message, the risk message was the next most preferred message, and the combination of the two was preferred the least. In addition to the feedback the influencers had to the message types that was discussed in Chapter 7, the influencers also had interesting thoughts specifically on the use of creative in both of those message types. This feedback provides some insights into what kinds of visuals influencers prefer and how powerful they can be.

In terms of the prevention message, while the majority of online influencers preferred this message overall, what was interesting is that use of visuals appeared to play only a minimal role in why they selected this particular message type. Rather, the informative value of it and its list format appeared to be what really drove the influencers to choose this message type.

On the other hand, as it relates to influencers' preference for the risk message type (and as we briefly discussed in Chapter 7), use of graphics does appear to be a main reason why influencers chose this one. In addition to the fact that influencers said this message type was more reader- and user-friendly, other select comments from online influencers who preferred this message type included "Images resonate better with my readers" and "Graphics are easier to skim and less intimidating". These comments further suggest that the risk message type used visuals well, which influencers felt would help convey complex information about Zika to their followers.

Inclusion of creative in content for influencers is not really an option anymore. They are a primary content type if you want to catch people's attention. Moreover, they help distill complex information—which is incredibly important when talking about health topics and trying to easily convey different health messages.

As you work with influencers to promote your programs, you will notice that they will want—and proactively seek out or create—interesting and engaging creative to include in their posts and to share in social media. To better prepare yourselves to be able to serve their needs, below are some creative content tips to consider.

Tips for Communicators

So creative is—or should be—a very important part of your content strategy, especially when working with influencers. They help convey data. They help communicate important information. They help with comprehension of complex issues. And they address the issue of our waning attention spans.

Static graphics are probably the easiest place to start if you are new to creative content development. If that is the case, consider the following best practices.

Create Unique Designs[109]

If you have graphics talent within your organization, program, or initiative, creating your own unique designs is one of the best things you can do to capture people's attention. Not only is it better than using stock photography because it will be more interesting to followers, but as well, it will be unique. And anything not shared broadly—anything that cannot be found elsewhere—is currency online and will help you successfully engage influencers. If they can share something no one else can, it will pique their—and their followers'—interest.

Make Text the Focus of Your Social Media Graphic Design

Use of block text in combination with a visual is becoming increasingly popular and more recognized among general consumers with the emergence of popular GIFs and memes (as we discussed earlier). When designing your graphics, consider connecting short and smart text to your visual to communicate your point. This can also help with accessibility for people with visual impairments.

If All Else Fails, Stock Photography and Icons Can Spruce Up Your Visual Content

I know, creating your own graphics may sound expensive and time-intensive so if you do not have the skills or budget to design your own graphics, stock photography can be used. Even better is to use icons, which can easily be found in traditional computer software programs. As well, there are social media templates out there that you can use to get started if you do not have access to advanced graphic skills. Canva[110] and CreativeMarket[111] are just two platforms that provide these templates.

Keep the Platform in Mind

It is important to note that not all content works the same way across all platforms. Below are some heuristics, as of the publication of this book, that you can follow when creating content for use in social media.

- Facebook[112]
  - Shared Image: 1,200 × 630 pixels
  - The image cannot be more than 20% text
- Twitter[113]
  - 1,024 pixels wide by 512 pixels (a maximum 5 MB file size for photos)
  - On desktop devices, Twitter images appear in the timeline at 506 pixels wide by 253 pixels tall so make sure that if the image is cropped, you can still see the text
  - Maintain the 2:1 ratio of the images, which can be reduced to a smaller version to fit in a follower's Twitter stream
- Instagram[114]
  - Portrait Size is recommended, which is 1,080 × 1,350 pixels

Maybe you are not interested in static graphics—or maybe you've got graphics covered for your initiative or program. That is great. If that is the case and you are interested in working more with video content, consider the following best practices.

Focus on the Story[115]

We've talked about the value of personal narrative in creating compelling content. This holds true for video as well. Consider what story you want to tell with your video—it should not just be a bunch of talking heads on screen, but it should take the viewer on a journey.

Keep It Short

Social media is all about instant gratification. Moreover, we now know that our attention spans are waning. In fact, marketers usually only have about 10 seconds to capture people's attention. So you need to give viewers what they are seeking quickly and easily.

Therefore, consider the length of your video when creating it. You want to get your main point out immediately so that viewers see it before they drop off and stop watching. As well, you will need to adhere to the specific specifications of the platform where the video will be placed. Recommended video lengths by platform can be found in Table 8.1.

Table 8.1 Recommended Video Lengths by Platform

- Instagram: 26 seconds
- Twitter: 45 seconds
- Facebook: 1 minutes
- YouTube: 2 minutes

Be Relevant

This is key. You do not want to try and appeal to everyone with just one video. I know that that sounds resource-intensive—but by trying to be everything to everyone in one video, you run the risk of being nothing to no one. And then, you've just wasted your resources. A better approach is to create multiple short videos (instead of one longer one) that speak to unique subgroups and on individual topics.

Descriptions are Everything

Video descriptions may seem like an afterthought to some, but they are important. Do not skimp on writing these kinds of descriptions. They provide the viewer with a quick idea of what the video is all about, and they help with search engine optimization (SEO) because the descriptions help your video show up in Google and YouTube search results.

A final note here is on branding. Across all of your creative—graphic, video, or otherwise—make sure to stick with your brand's unique visual esthetic. That means that everything should be using the same fonts, colors, logos, and types of photos. That way, if someone sees your creative in multiple places, they know that they are related and belong to the same family of materials, and to your brand. It also helps hammer the message home—this is all part of one message and one initiative.

Final Reflections

In conclusion, as we said earlier, it is not just about considering whether to use creative in your messaging nowadays, it is a requirement to do so. Creative *needs* to be a part of your content strategy.

Funny and smart visuals can enhance your message, when done right, drawing viewers in and capturing their attention. The story that we started this chapter with about Pregnant Chicken's post exemplifies how this approach can be implemented successfully.

But it is also important to consider the different types of visuals and creative that are available and can be included in your content. Using a variety of types of creative can help keep things fresh and interesting and provide options for your influencers to choose from.

While creative can be used across platforms, we know that these need to be tailored to the specific platform where they will be used. As well, you may want to consider how your audiences differ across platforms and craft creative targeted to each subgroup by platform.

Moreover, keeping influencer preferences in mind as you develop your graphics will be key. Ask them questions. Show them your ideas and get their feedback. Crowdsourcing your ideas with the community you are seeking to engage is a great way to make sure you are developing great—not just good—creative.

As we saw with the Pregnant Chicken post, asking for input from online influencers to understand what works best with blog readers and social media followers is key. It makes for compelling ways to convey your message. It might not be how you would do it—but it works.

Doing this will ensure that you create something great right from the start. And it will also save you time and money because you know the creative will ultimately be used.

Conclusion

con·clu·sion | /kən'klo͞oZHən/ | noun
The last part of something.

Well, here we are. The end of the book. At the outset of this book, I laid out clear goals for what I wanted this book to be, and I hope it has lived up to your expectations. I guess if you made it this far and are reading this final chapter, it did.

We began this journey together with a story about why I do what I do and why I love what I do. I shared how social media changed my life—or rather, the life of my grandmother—and how, through that experience, I saw the power of online social networks to improve people's health and lives.

I shared how online influencers are critical to the future of social media, given the challenges that marketers are facing today. I also shared how for the last 10 years, I have been working with them to advance health outcomes for various populations. Seeing, firsthand, the successes that we have had together has resulted in my knowing them better, understanding them more, having a greater awareness of the context in which online influencers work (both individually and as part of a network), and being able to see the endless opportunities for how these layperson opinion leaders can impact lives for the better.

To help you understand where these digital opinion leaders even came from, we started, well, at the beginning. I shared how much of the power in social networks comes from the influence that opinion leaders wield. And how these opinion leaders come is all shapes and sizes and from all walks of life—but how what is consistent among them is the fact that they can sway popular opinion about all sorts of things, from books and movies to eating (or not eating) beef to using a condom.

Chapter 1 was a bit of theory, mixed with a bit of data, mixed with a bit of history. It aimed to set the foundation for why you should consider working with online influencers. Based in science, online influencers are the digital versions of everyday opinion leaders who have been both disrupting how innovations spread through communities and shaping conversations around health globally for decades now. Online influencers embody this same ideal but in a different medium—one that is digital—which is where people are primarily connecting and getting their information today.

In Chapter 2, we examined the influencer-follower relationship in more detail in order to better understand it. We discussed how they establish credibility and trust with their followers, and how this is what makes online influencers so persuasive.

Chapter 3 aimed to build on the lessons about the online influencer industry discussed in Chapters 1 and 2 by taking a closer look at this world of online influencers, how they work, how they network, and how an entire industry has been built on their existence.

Throughout Chapters 2 and 3, we also discussed how this space is shifting and becoming highly networked and increasingly monetized. We touched on how these changes are altering relationships with their followers and with other influencers, and how this is creating factions within the online influencer community.

For instance, some influencers are seriously focused on presenting a certain image to their followers—one that is pretty, perfect, and always curated—while others are railing against this perception of perfection and trying to maintain transparency and honesty with their followers and build closer relationships with other influencers.

Chapter 3 ended with some tips on how to identify and vet influencers and tips for engaging them.

It was my hope that the information shared up to this point would give you a good perspective of "who" these online influencers are and "why" they are incredibly influential to others. And with this more general foundation of the online influencer world now set, we could begin to examine the interplay of online influencers and the world of health.

In Chapter 4, we discussed how online influencers think about communicating about health. We discussed their need to position a health topic within the context of their own blog and social media—so that it fits and makes sense to them and to their followers. We also looked at how the worlds of online influencers and health need each other. They need each other to share accurate information. They need each other to avoid sharing misinformation. They need each other to save lives.

Finally, we discussed in Chapter 4 how there is a lack of understanding among some influencers about where health *could* fit into their blog or social media content. Some influencers just have not yet considered that health could align with the content they are already writing about when it is not already focused on health. I concluded this chapter with some ideas about where various health topics might fit into different genres of topics that influencers write about.

To understand this phenomenon a bit more, we examined risk in Chapter 5—what it is and how both influencers and brands think about it. I shared with you how my research elucidated that online influencers tend to be risk-averse. They see their blogs and social media profiles as their happy places, and they do not really want to invite too much controversy into those spaces.

While this may seem like a non-starter as it relates to health, I also shared that there are aspects of influencers' lives and interests that will influence how they perceive the risk of communicating about a health topic and make them more willing to do so. Examples include a sense of altruism and a personal connection to a health issue.

In Chapter 6, we talked about fatalism, as a social influence that governs our thinking and behaviors. We discussed what fatalism is and how it influences our behaviors—especially our behaviors about health. I shared with you that my research found that this community of online influencers is not particularly fatalistic and how that is an opportunity for marketers.

In Chapter 7, we built on this finding by examining a few remarkable examples of influencers who have struggled with health issues but still feel compelled to be engaged in their own health and share health information with their followers. Central to this is their common belief that "there are things we can all do to take better care of ourselves." This sense of self-efficacy that they exhibit in spite of the challenges that they face suggests that there are many opportunities to overcome existing barriers and engage online influencers to share health information.

At this point in the book, we had a good sense that online influencers are interested in and motivated to share health information, and that they are not deterred by social norms, such as fatalism, in doing so. But we also had established that influencers' brands and reputations are of the utmost importance to them, and that this, in turn, determines the kinds of content they are willing to share.

This suggested to us that messaging and creative were important components of working with influencers on health topics and made these topics worthy of some discussion. This brought us to Chapters 7 and 8, where we reviewed influencer preferences for health messages and perspectives on using different types of creative content, respectively.

We also talked about using simple language, but not dumbing down your message. We talked about how our attention spans are waning and how we need to find ways to convey important information quickly and easily. We talked about strategies for getting your message right with influencers as well as how to create great visuals that make it easy for influencers to share your messages online.

Throughout this book, I have shared some really personal stories with you. Some had to do with online influencers, specifically, while others had to do with opinion leaders more generally. Some had to do with health, while others had nothing to do with health. Some of these stories are moving, while others embarrassing. Some of these stories are my own, and some of them are from others whom I have had the pleasure to meet throughout my work.

All of these stories have moved me—whether mine or others'. Because they convey influencers' personal trials with health. Because they are stories of bravery. And because these influencers have been willing to be transparent and honest with me about very sensitive topics.

These stories are meant to be guide posts for you to help you remember key points from this book. I mean, I want you to remember it all, for sure, but I also know how I work and how I learn—and recall—information. For me, lessons that are taught through storytelling are often recalled *much better* than just remembering data and facts. As you ponder the information shared in this book, I hope that these stories resonate with you well into the future and help you recall key points about working with online influencers as you need them.

So we've come to the end of the book. But, hopefully, it is actually just the beginning for you in your work with influencers.

I want to thank Laura and Lisa, Carol and Elle, Monique, Sue, Sarah, Molly, and ALL the influencers who talked with me as part of my research, who have worked with me over the years, and who shared their stories with me—so poignant and so personal. I have the utmost respect for these influencers and the work they continue to do for themselves, their followers, and their communities.

I hope this book has given you the foundation and the tools to help you in your work with online influencers. I hope this book has inspired you to work a little bit more in this world. I hope this book has motivated you to try and use these trusted voices to improve lives.

Trust me, if you invest in them, they will invest in you. And it is worth it.

Notes

1 www.statita.com/statistics/282087/number-of-monthly-active-twitter-users/.
2 https://blog.hubspot.com/marketing/facebook-organic-reach-declining.
3 https://en.wikipedia.org/wiki/Ad_blocking.
4 www.mediapost.com/publications/article/315291/spotlight-on-ad-blocking-awareness-of-new-chrome.html.
5 https://performancein.com/news/2017/12/29/pi-predictions-2018-will-be-the-year-influencer/.
6 https://performancein.com/news/2018/01/24/sponsored-instagram-posts-reached-15-million-globally-2017/.
7 http://theinspirationroom.com/daily/2009/geico-gecko-on-youtube/.
8 www.americashealthrankings.org/explore/annual.
9 Statista.com. Number of social media users worldwide from 2010 to 2020 (in billions). Accessed at: www.statista.com/statistics/278414/number-of-worldwide-social-network-users/.
10 www.centerforfoodsafety.org/issues/1040/mad-cow-disease/timeline-mad-cow-disease-outbreaks.
11 http://content.time.com/time/specials/packages/article/0,28804,1939460_1939452_1939475,00.html.
12 www.usatoday.com/story/life/tv/2015/10/19/oprah-effect-does-everything-she-touches-turn-gold/74211636/.
13 http://jur.byu.edu/?p=5599.
14 www.ncbi.nlm.nih.gov/books/NBK384914/ accessed on July 25, 2018.

15 http://sphweb.bumc.bu.edu/otlt/MPH-Modules/SB/BehavioralChangeTheories/BehavioralChangeTheories7.html accessed on July 25, 2018.
16 www.sciencedirect.com/science/article/pii/S0277953608001512 accessed on July 25, 2018.
17 Katz, E., & Lazarsfeld, P. F. (1957). *Personal influence.* New York: Free Press.
18 Rogers, E. M. (2010). *Diffusion of innovations.* Simon and Schuster.
19 Kinnunen, J. (1996). Gabriel Tarde as a founding father of innovation diffusion research. *Acta sociologica, 39*(4), 431–442.
20 Puska, P., Koskela, K., McAlister, A., Mäyränen, H., Smolander, A., Moisio, S., Viri, L., Korpelainen, V., & Rogers, E. M. (1986). Use of lay opinion leaders to promote diffusion of health innovations in a community programme: lessons learned from the North Karelia project. *Bulletin of the World Health Organization, 64*(3), 437.
21 O'brien, D. J., Hassinger, E. W., Brown, R. B., & Pinkerton, J. R. (1991). The social networks of leaders in more and less viable rural communities 1. *Rural Sociology, 56*(4), 699–716.
22 https://www.ncbi.nlm.nih.gov/pmc/articles/PMC2957672/.
23 Valente, T. W., & Pumpuang, P. (2007). Identifying opinion leaders to promote behavior change. *Health Education & Behavior, 34*(6), 881–896.
24 www.pewinternet.org/fact-sheet/social-media/.
25 Burke-Garcia, A. (2017). *Opinion Leaders for Health: Formative Research with Bloggers about Health Information Dissemination* (Doctoral dissertation, George Mason University).
26 Huffaker, D. (2010). Dimensions of leadership and social influence in online communities. *Human Communication Research, 36*(4), 593–617.
27 Winterich, K. P., Gangwar, M., & Grewal, R. (2018). When celebrities count: power distance beliefs and celebrity endorsements. *Journal of Marketing, 82*(3), 70–86.
28 Atkin, C., & Block, M. (1983). Effectiveness of celebrity endorsers. *Journal of Advertising Research*, 23(1), 57–61.
29 Aziz, S., Ghani, U., & Niazi, A. (2013). Impact of celebrity credibility on advertising effectiveness. *Pakistan Journal of Commerce & Social Sciences, 7*(1).

30 Goldsmith, R. E., Lafferty, B. A., & Newell, S. J. (2000). The impact of corporate credibility and celebrity credibility on consumer reaction to advertisements and brands. *Journal of Advertising, 29*(3), 43–54.
31 www.publishersweekly.com/pw/by-topic/childrens/childrens-industry-news/article/49213-the-mighty-mom-bloggers.html.
32 https://moodle.queenelizabeth.cumbria.sch.uk/pluginfile.php/238490/mod_resource/content/0/136%20The%20Rise%20of%20YouTube%20Opinion%20Leaders.pdf.
33 Hwang, K., & Zhang, Q. (2018). Influence of parasocial relationship between digital celebrities and their followers on followers' purchase and electronic word-of-mouth intentions, and persuasion knowledge. Computers in Human Behavior, 87, 155-173.
34 https://dooce.com/about/.
35 www.thecut.com/2015/05/dooce-talks-life-after-mommy-blogging.html.
36 http://time.com/money/5269576/mommy-bloggers-success/.
37 https://dooce.com/2009/02/19/lipstick-on-a-pig/.
38 https://dooce.com/2007/12/13/because-i-couldnt-say-it-on-the-phone/.
39 https://dooce.com/2004/08/28/unlocked/.
40 https://medium.com/crobox/under-the-influence-the-power-of-social-media-influencers-5192571083c3.
41 https://medium.com/ama-marketing-news/what-every-marketer-needs-to-know-about-influencer-marketing-and-buying-followers-31d5d64ce1a1.
42 https://adage.com/article/digital/study-influencer-spenders-finds-big-names-fake-followers/313223/.
43 https://spinsucks.com/communication/fake-influencer-marketing/.
44 Granovetter, M. S. (1977). The strength of weak ties. In *Social networks* (pp. 347–367).
45 www.forbes.com/sites/forbesagencycouncil/2018/12/28/10-improvements-influencer-marketing-has-to-make-in-2019/#41b353b44044.
46 www.statista.com/statistics/427309/influencer-marketing-emv-by-industry/.
47 Personal conversation, Cooper Munroe, September 18, 2018.
48 www.socialbakers.com/blog/2660–8-reasons-why-you-should-attend-social-media-conferences.

49 www.theleverageway.com/blog/influencer-marketing-on-facebook/.
50 https://support.google.com/adsense/answer/6242051?hl=en
51 Libai, B., Biyalogorsky, E., & Gerstner, E. (2003). Setting referral fees in affiliate marketing. *Journal of Service Research, 5*(4), 303–315, p. 303.
52 www.themotherhood.com/ftc-disclosure-guidelines/.
53 www.emarketer.com/Report/Influencer-Marketing-2018-Why-Disclosure-Mustand-How-Branded-Content-Tools-Fit/2002202.
54 www.mommymafia.com/.
55 www.theleverageway.com/blog/influencer-identification-tools-find-brand-partners/.
56 www.hacscrap.com/search?q=scrapbooking&x=0&y=0.
57 McCroskey, J. C. (1992). Reliability and validity of the willingness to communicate scale. *Communication Quarterly, 40*(1), 16–25.
58 Wiese, J., Kelley, P. G., Cranor, L. F., Dabbish, L., Hong, J. I., & Zimmerman, J. (2011, September). Are you close with me? are you nearby?: investigating social groups, closeness, and willingness to share. In *Proceedings of the 13th international conference on Ubiquitous computing* (pp. 197–206). ACM.
59 Wright, K. B., Frey, L., & Sopory, P. (2007). Willingness to communicate about health as an underlying trait of patient self-advocacy: The development of the willingness to communicate about health (WTCH) measure. *Communication Studies, 58*(1), 35–51.
60 Wright K, Fisher C, Rising C, Burke-Garcia A, Afanaseva D, & Cai X. (2018). Partnering with mommy bloggers to disseminate breast cancer risk information: a social media intervention (preprint). *Journal of Medical Internet Research.*
61 Burke-Garcia, A., Berry, C. N., Kreps, G. L., & Wright, K. B. (2017, January). The power & perspective of Mommy Bloggers: Formative research with social media opinion leaders about HPV vaccination. In *Proceedings of the 50th Hawaii International Conference on System Sciences.*
62 Nardi, B. A., Schiano, D. J., Gumbrecht, M., & Swartz, L. (2004). Why we blog. *Communications of the ACM, 47*(12), 41–46, p. 42.
63 Lenhart, A., & Fox, S. (2006). Bloggers. Pew Research Center. Accessed at www.pewinternet.org/2006/07/19/bloggers/ on April 1, 2017.

64 Lopez, L. K. (2009). The radical act of 'mommy blogging': redefining motherhood through the blogosphere. *New Media & Society, 11*(5), 729–747.
65 Risk, A., & Petersen, C. (2002). Health information on the internet: quality issues and international initiatives. *JAMA, 287*(20), 2713–2715.
66 https://medium.com/ama-marketing-news/how-to-host-an-engaging-social-media-chat-and-keep-the-trolls-at-bay-b48736abedc0.
67 Seeman, N., Ing, A., & Rizo, C. (2010). Assessing and responding in real time to online anti-vaccine sentiment during a flu pandemic. *Healthc Q, 13*(Sp), 8–15.
68 Keelan, J., Pavri-Garcia, V., Tomlinson, G., & Wilson, K. (2007). YouTube as a source of information on immunization: a content analysis. *JAMA, 298*(21), 2482–2484.
69 https://scholarspace.manoa.hawaii.edu/bitstream/10125/41388/1/paper0239.pdf.
70 https://stylebyemilyhenderson.com/blog/7-things-learned-posting-photo-obama-random-saturday-night-losing-4k-instagram-followers.
71 https://stylebyemilyhenderson.com/blog/7-things-learned- posting-photo-obama-random-saturday-night-losing-4k-instagram-followers.
72 www.jdentaled.org/content/jde/65/10/1007.full.pdf.
73 Witte, K., Meyer, G., & Martell, D. (2001). *Effective health risk messages: A step-by-step guide.* Sage.
74 Perloff, R. M. (2003). The dynamics of persuasion. In *Communication and attitude in the 21st century.* Hillsdale, NJ: LawrenceIbErbaum.
75 www.uky.edu/~ngrant/CJT780/readings/Day%209/Witte1992.pdf.
76 www.webmd.com/a-to-z-guides/ehlers-danlos-syndrome-facts.
77 Powe, B. D., & Weinrich, S. (1999, April). An intervention to decrease cancer fatalism among rural elders. In *Oncology nursing forum* (Vol. 26, No. 3, pp. 583–588).
78 Niederdeppe, J., & Levy, A. G. (2007). Fatalistic beliefs about cancer prevention and three prevention behaviors. *Cancer Epidemiology and Prevention Biomarkers, 16*(5), 998–1003.
79 Powe, B. D. (1996). Cancer fatalism among African-Americans: a review of the literature. *Nursing outlook, 44*(1), 18–21.
80 Perez-Stable, E. J., Sabogal, F., Otero-Sabogal, R., Hiatt, R. A., & McPhee, S. J. (1992). Misconceptions about cancer among Latinos and Anglos. *JAMA, 268*(22), 3219–3223.

81 www.alanberkowitz.com/articles/social_norms.pdf accessed on July 25, 2018.
82 Straughan, P. T., & Seow, A. (1998). Fatalism reconceptualized: a concept to predict health screening behavior. *Journal of Gender, Culture and Health, 3*(2), 85–100.
83 www.uky.edu/~eushe2/Bandura/Bandura1990EPP.pdf.
84 www.cdc.gov/flu/protect/vaccine/quadrivalent.htm.
85 http://time.com/3858309/attention-spans-goldfish/.
86 www.plainlanguage.gov/guidelines/audience/.
87 www.plainlanguage.gov/guidelines/words/.
88 www.plainlanguage.gov/guidelines/organize/.
89 https://crowdriff.com/blog/visual-marketing-statistics/.
90 https://crowdriff.com/blog/examples-visual-influencer-brands-dmos/.
91 www.pewinternet.org/2013/10/28/photo-and-video-sharing-grow-online-2/.
92 www.thedrum.com/news/2015/04/24/facebook-influences-over-half-shoppers-says-digitaslbi-s-connected-commerce-report.
93 www.journalism.org/.
94 www.socialreport.com/insights/article/360000663006-7-Digital-Marketing-Trends-That-Will-Own-2019.
95 www.business2community.com/social-media/the-top-7-social-media-marketing-trends-going-into-2019-02119776.
96 www.businessinsider.com/youtube-user-statistics-2018-5.
97 https://smartslider3.com/youtube-slider/.
98 https://buffer.com/library/instagram-stories.
99 http://nymag.com/intelligencer/2018/10/instagram-igtv-flop.html.
100 www.forbes.com/sites/jaysondemers/2016/04/26/facebook-live-everything-you-need-to-know/#2f47bcdd55f2.
101 www.facebook.com/facebookmedia/blog/tips-for-using-live.
102 www.engadget.com/2018/04/06/facebook-live-2-year-statistics/.
103 https://knowyourmeme.com/memes/people/richard-dawkins.
104 https://academic.oup.com/jcmc/article/20/4/417/4067574.
105 https://knowyourmeme.com/.
106 www.nytimes.com/2014/11/06/business/media/teenage-clerk-rises-from-target-to-star-on-twitter-and-talk-shows-.html.
107 https://searchbusinessanalytics.techtarget.com/definition/data-visualization.
108 www.sas.com/en_in/insights/big-data/data-visualization.html.
109 https://venngage.com/blog/social-media-graphic-design/.
110 www.canva.com/templates/social-graphics/.

111 https://creativemarket.com/templates/social-media.
112 www.contentharmony.com/blog/facebook-ads-20-percent-grid-template/.
113 https://buffer.com/library/twitter-images.
114 https://support.sendible.com/hc/en-us/articles/115005459463-Recommended-image-and-video-formats-for-Instagram.
115 www.moovly.com/blog/top-6-tips-for-creating-a-successful-social-video-the-rise-of-video-marketing.

Index

T

U

V

W

Y

Z

Printed in the United States
by Baker & Taylor Publisher Services